TIJERINA AND THE LAND GRANTS

"If the Treaty is valid enforce it. If it is not,
the United States is trespassing in the Southwest."
—REIES LOPEZ TIJERINA

Reies Tijerina and his wife, Patsy, leaving Albuquerque district court after acquittal of charges stemming from Tierra Amarilla Courthouse raid, December 1968.

TIJERINA
and the
LAND GRANTS

Mexican Americans in
Struggle for Their Heritage

by Patricia Bell Blawis

INTERNATIONAL PUBLISHERS

New York

To Jack

who helped write this book

Library of Congress Card Catalog Number: 79-175178
ISBN (Cloth) 0-7178-0336-8; (paperback) 0-7178-0337-6
Printed in the United States of America

Contents

GLOSSARY

Alianza	Alliance
Alianzista	Member of the Alliance
Anglo	Person of an English-speaking culture
Aztlán	Nahuatl name meaning "The lands to the north:" thus, the present Southwestern states of the United States
Barrio	Neighborhood or ghetto
Chicano	A Mexican resident of the United States
Contratista	Labor contractors who transport Mexican workers, hire them out to farmers, and take part of their pay
Corrido	Topical song, ballad
Ejido	A communal system of land tenure
Macho, machismo	Male, male dominance
Merced	A land grant
Mestizo	Of Indian and Spanish heritage
Vendido	A betrayer—one who has sold out

TERMS

Various names are used to identify the Mexican minority in the United States. Along the border, the ancient term "Mexican" was stripped of its dignity by the ruling Anglos, so Mexican people often sought descriptions that avoided the terms "Spanish American," "Spanish Speaking," and so on.

In this country, U.S. citizens of Mexican descent usually speak of themselves in Spanish as *"Mexicanos"* or *"Raza."* The latter term encompasses all New World, Spanish-speaking peoples. "Chicano," most popular among militants, is derived from the word "Mexicano."

Tijerina prefers "Indo-Hispano," which indicates the fusion of cultures of the people in this area. This book is about Tijerina, so the author uses his term. But, speaking of himself, Reies has always said, *"Soy Mexicano"*—I am a Mexican.

Preface

WHEN THE daughter of "Corky" Gonzales was married at a Denver conference of Chicano youth, the priest blessed her in the name of the God of Che, the God of Reies Tijerina, and the God of César Chavez: placing Reies Lopez Tijerina in the center of the new and vigorous Chicano movements for equality with the dominant Anglo.

Tijerina has been in the center of this fight since a summer afternoon in 1967, when heirs to land grants in New Mexico took over a courthouse—an outburst that sent echoes around the world. In every *barrio* from San Antonio to Denver and Los Angeles, Tijerina became the symbol of the rage of this oppressed national minority—ten million people who earn less, are unemployed twice as often, and have ten years less of life than the rest of the population.

The recourse Tijerina demands for the problems of his people challenges the basic assumptions on which the Southwest has been ruled for 123 years. The war the United States waged against Mexico to conquer a vast territory, also engulfed the Mexican population who lived there. They became a conquered people, and state and federal authorities still work together to keep them conquered. Only theoretically have they been extended the full rights of U.S. citizenship guaranteed them in the peace of Guadalupe Hidalgo that concluded the war.

Tijerina has revived efforts to enforce this treaty, with emphasis on the fundamental question of land tenure. Going back to the original deeds by Spain and Mexico, he put the fight to regain the communal grants on a firm legal foundation, and thereby provoked the anger of the powerful.

This book follows the career of Tijerina up to the present time, a man who met racial oppression from his earliest childhood as a migrant farm worker. We shall observe the ways he found of fighting it and leading others in the fight, first in the isolation of his own national group, then gradually in the recognition that a common front of all hurt by racism, including the "good Anglos," is what must bring the monster down.

July 19, 1971   P.B.B.

1. The War Against Mexico

THE OPPRESSION of the Indo-Hispanic people of the Southwest began with the war against Mexico. Spain's legacies of New Mexico, Texas and California lay across the path of the former English colonies as they extended westward. Since 1821 these lands had belonged to Mexico, which had freed itself from Spain. But, Mexican legal claims to the territories did not curb the appetite of the Anglo-Americans.

ANNEXATION OF TEXAS

INFILTRATION OF the Mexican state of Texas had begun even before Mexican independence. Under the "liberal" constitution granted by Spain in 1820, Moses Austin of Louisiana obtained a concession for 300 families. Every colonist was to receive 640 acres for himself, plus 320 acres for his wife, 100 for each child and 40 for each slave. In return for the right to settle, he pledged allegiance to the Spanish crown. When Moses Austin died, his son Stephen traveled to Mexico to confirm the concession with the newly established Mexican government. He succeeded in increasing it to 2,000 families. Indeed, within ten years there were 20,000 immigrants from the United States in Texas.

The cotton economy of the U.S. immigrants depended entirely on slave labor. Thus, the question of slavery was the key to the history of Texas from the time the first U.S. immigrant entered until slavery was abolished in the United States.*

* The British commission for the suppression of the slave trade reported that in 1837–38 no less than 15,000 slaves from Africa were brought into Texas.[1]

The slave power has been blamed both for the theft of Texas and the war against Mexico. But racist attitudes were not confined, as some suppose, to the slave-state politicians. The assumption of natural superiority over the Hispano-American appeared even in the thinking of men like Thomas Jefferson or John Quincy Adams.*

When the Mexican state of Coahuila-Texas established a constitution abolishing slavery, "the screams of the slave owners reached to the skies."[3] In 1833 Stephen Austin again traveled to Mexico City with a proposal to separate Texas from Coahuila and form another state. He threatened that the government of Texas would be overthrown by the Anglo colonists if these terms were not agreed to.

The armed revolt of the Anglo-Americans defeated the Mexican forces under General Santa Anna at the battle of San Jacinto in April 1836. Santa Anna was captured and signed away Texas to his captors, but, as soon as he set foot on Mexican soil he repudiated the agreement. However, he was unable to continue the war effort because the Church, controlling three-quarters of all Mexican resources, did not offer assistance. In addition, the feudal landowners were as proslavery as those of Texas.

Since a peace treaty was never negotiated, no boundaries between the two nations had been fixed. Texas claimed all the territory to the Río Grande; Mexico insisted that the boundary rested on the Nueces.† Mexico continued to occupy

* Jefferson had written in 1823 that he long thought Cuba would make "an interesting acquisition for the United States." In 1825 J. Q. Adams had proposed the purchase of Texas from Mexico. President Adams advised his envoy, Joel Poinsett, to urge the deal on the Mexicans with the argument that by making the sale, their national capital would be nearer the center of their country. This insult by the "blue-eyed buffaloes" is recalled by Mexicans to this day.[2]

† The Secretary of Foreign Affairs of Mexico, Don Manuel C. Rejón, stated (October 20, 1844) that "when a nation attempts to annex territories to stain them with the slavery of an unfortunate branch of the human family, the aggrieved nation has the right to make efforts to limit

the strip between the Nueces and the Río Grande, and "in the bloody zone between the two rivers an uninterrupted guerrilla warfare continued throughout the life of the Texas Republic."[4]

At the same time, there was a strong movement in the Republic of Texas for annexation to the United States. By early 1845 the annexation had been voted by the U.S. Congress and had been confirmed in July by the Texas Congress.

INVASION OF MEXICO

WITH TEXAS now a state, the U.S. government was in a position to press the boundary claims of the Republic of Texas. In an effort to provoke the Mexican government into a conflict President Polk moved to occupy Mexican lands south of the Nueces. He sent Major General Zachary Taylor with between 3,000 and 4,000 troops to Corpus Christi. The U.S. Army entered territory which Texas had never controlled. Before the end of 1845, Taylor was ordered across the Nueces strip and right up to the Rio Grande. Still, the Mexican authorities had offered no opposition.

Finally, in April of 1846 Taylor blockaded the mouth of the Río Grande. This outright act of war was met with a reprisal by the Mexican army. When the news reached Washington, President Polk, tired of waiting, was already preparing his war message to Congress. This latest information gave him the opportunity he sought.

"The cup of forbearance had been exhausted," wrote the President who had done everything to make war certain. "Now after reiterated menaces, Mexico has passed the boundary of the United States, has invaded our territory and shed *American blood upon the American soil.* As war exists, and

the expansion of territory in which this abominable traffic is carried on. Let us leave it to the world to decide on whose side reason and justice lies."[5]

notwithstanding all our efforts to avoid it, exists by act of Mexico herself . . . I invoke the prompt action of Congress.

The House vote was 173 to 14, that of the Senate 42 to 2.* One of the opposing members of the House, Alexander H. Stephens of Georgia, would soon name the President, "Polk the Mendacious." Henry Clay, the leader of the opposition party, said that the war bill had "a palpable falsehood stamped upon its face. All the nations, I apprehend, look upon us, in the prosecution of the present war, as being actuated by a spirit of rapacity, and an inordinate desire for territorial aggrandizement."[7]

The U.S. military launched a three-pronged attack against Mexico. General Taylor was ordered to seize Monterey and move toward Mexico City from the north. General Winfield Scott would capture Vera Cruz and march on Mexico City from the south. Colonel S. W. Kearny was assigned the occupation of the New Mexican territory.

The U.S. forces held superior military might and mounted an all-out offensive throughout Mexico. But the course of the war was also determined by the interests of the landlord and clerical circles that ruled Mexico. These groups would tolerate any invader sooner than the invasion of their own privileges. They feared the Mexican peasant more than anyone else, and had seen to it that he was not armed. Since it was these very people who were called on to fight the U.S. troops, the treason of the Mexican ruling class proved disastrous for

---

* The House itself, before the war was over, would resolve (in January 1848) that Polk had begun the war "unnecessarily and unconstitutionally." A one-term member from Illinois, Abraham Lincoln, would join the attack. U. S. Grant, then a young officer under General Taylor, wrote of the conflict: "We were sent to provoke a fight, but it was essential that Mexico should commence it. . . . The occupation, separation, and annexation were, from the inception of the movement to its final consummation, a conspiracy to acquire territory out of which slave states might be formed for the American Union. Even if the annexation itself could be justified, the manner in which the subsequent war was forced on Mexico cannot."[6]

Mexico.* In fact, as the U.S. forces penetrated deeper into Mexican territory, the peasants assumed the brunt of the popular resistance. Reactionary Mexicans viewed a U.S. victory with relief, as they would the French invasion and the "Emperor" Maximilian in the 1860s.

The U.S. government actively sought to inflame the antagonisms between the various ruling groups. For example, Polk was in secret communication with Santa Anna, exiled in Cuba at the outbreak of war. Polk allowed him to pass through the U.S. naval blockade to return to Mexico, where he was given command of the forces being raised to meet the northern invasion under Taylor. Santa Anna organized and trained these troops with ability, and marching them north, met Taylor at Angostura on February 22, 1847. After two days of fighting the Mexicans had gained the advantage when Santa Anna inexplicably abandoned the battle and marched back toward San Luis Potosí.

Although General Taylor's campaign met serious obstacles, General Scott was able to penetrate from Vera Cruz to Mexico City during the summer of 1847. His forces captured the Vera Cruz Custom House, the principle source of income for the Mexican government. There were several serious engagements on the road to Mexico City at Cerro Gordo, Contreras and Churubusco. The last stand took place at the hill-top castle of Chapultepec above Mexico City, the Mexican national military school, whose cadets were ordered by Santa Anna to leave before the attack. They refused, fought to the bitter end, and became the Niños Heroes of the National Pantheon.

The capitulation of the official resistance to the invasion was followed by an outflowing of popular resistance. The Mexican poor opposed the U.S. forces with virtually no arms.

* "The Mexican peoples' failure in the struggle is attributed not only to the economic and military superiority of the U.S., but, to a considerable extent, to the anti-patriotic activities of the Mexican ruling class seeking to retain their own privileged positions at the expense of the national interest."[8]

"The people poured in, fired by rebellion. They poured bricks from the roof tops, attracted soldiers into *cul de sacs* and beat them."[9] Fifteen thousand unarmed men threw themselves against the invaders. In retaliation, many Mexicans were tortured in the public square and flogged to death by the U.S. command.

SEIZURE OF NEW MEXICO

THE THIRD U.S. force under Colonel Kearny began its offensive down the Santa Fe trail, with New Mexico, then a Department of Mexico, as its objective. To meet this crisis, the Governor of New Mexico, Don Manuel Armijo, gathered 4,000 volunteers at Santa Fe. But the treasury was depleted as a result of expenditures made five years earlier to repel an invasion from Texas. Armijo appealed to the large property owners to finance the defense of the territory. "If we are not able to preserve the integrity of our territory, all of Mexico will soon be the prey of the greed of our neighbors of the north."[10] Again, the feudal landowners refused to defend the interests of the nation as a whole. Armijo fled Santa Fe and the city was easily taken by the U.S. forces.

When the U.S. Army first marched into Santa Fe, the soldiers found it had "a foreign aspect in all respects."[11] The ancient city is built around a shady plaza, on one side of which stand the long, low walls of the Governor's Palace, built of adobe five feet thick. The life of the Palace centered around an enclosed courtyard, or patio, in the style Spain learned from earlier invaders, the Moors.

Santa Fe is seven thousand feet high, and surrounded by mountains green with piñon, a dwarf pine whose nuts are still gathered by Mexican families roaming across the hills in the bright autumn, when the city is at its sunny best. It is then that the people of Santa Fe hold their Fiesta in the Plaza.

But in the fall of 1846, there was no celebration to greet the invaders. One of them wrote home: "Our march into the city was extremely warlike, with drawn sabres and daggers in every look. Black eyes looked through latticed windows, some filled with tears . . . a wail of grief arose above the din of our horses' tread."[12]

The governor having fled, it was left to his lieutenant, Juan Bautista Vigil, to express the peoples' mood of resignation in his "welcoming" address to Kearny.

"No one in this world can successfully resist the power of him who is stronger. Do not find it strange if there has been no manifestation of joy and enthusiasm in seeing this city occupied by your military forces. To us the power of the Mexican Republic is dead. What child will not shed abundant tears at the tomb of his parents?"[13]

New Mexico would have its resistance yet. In December 1846, preparations for revolt were reported to Colonel Sterling Price, who had succeeded Kearny when the latter left for California. Humiliated by Armijo's surrender without a struggle, two prominent citizens, Tomás Ortiz and Diego Archuleta, organized an uprising together with Father Antonio José Martinez, the priest, teacher and author of Táos. Ortiz and Archuleta disappeared when the plans were revealed to the U.S. authorities.

In Colonel Price's words, reporting to the adjutant-general: "After the flight of Ortiz and Archuleta, the rebellion appeared to be suppressed, but this appearance was deceptive. On 14 January, Gov. Bent* left this city for Táos. On the 19th, this valuable officer, together with five other persons, were seized by the Pueblos and Mexicans, and were murdered. . . . On the same day, seven Americans were murdered at Arroyo Hondo, and two others on the Río Colorado." The rebels also shot several collaborators. "It ap-

---

* Less than a month after taking Santa Fe, Kearny appointed Charles Bent to serve as governor. A southerner, Bent's attitude toward his new constituents was summed up in a letter to his brother: "The Mexican character is made up of stupidity, obstinacy, ignorance, duplicity and vanity."

peared," wrote Col. Price, "to be the object of the insurrectionists to put to death every Mexican who had accepted office under the American government."

But soldiers' cannon prevailed over patriots' muskets, and in reprisal more than 30 Mexican and Indian leaders of the revolt were executed, charged with "treason" by the army of occupation. A noteworthy feature of the Táos Rebellion, as it was named although it spread far beyond Táos, was the joint resistance of Mexicans and Indians to the U.S. invader. This included not only the Pueblos, with whom the Mexicans normally coexisted, but the Apaches, who were at times hostile to both Pueblos and Mexicans.

THE VIRGIN'S TREATY

As THE course of the war widened on the three fronts and popular resistance increased, President Polk was faced with the possibility of a double disaster. There could be an open rebellion in Congress with a refusal to vote for war funds. Secondly, the increase in popular resistance by Mexicans raised the prospects of a long drawn-out occupation. Therefore, half way through the war, Polk had already sent the chief clerk of the State Department, Nicholas Trist, to negotiate a treaty with the Mexican government. Polk "had a firm, not to say convulsive, hold on his objectives: Upper California first, and New Mexico* in addition."[14]

A year later, having taken Mexico City, the President demanded an even greater portion of Mexico than called for in Trist's original instructions. He now laid claim to the northern tier of Mexico's states, and Lower (Baja) California as well. Trist ignored the new orders, and proceeded to negotiate the Treaty of Guadalupe Hidalgo† on the basis of Polk's

---

* Until 1863 New Mexico included the present state of Arizona.
† The wily Trist had selected the town dedicated to the Virgin of Guadalupe (Mexico's patron saint) as the site for signing the pact, in

minimum demands of a year earlier. Although infuriated, the President sent Trist's treaty to the Senate with a recommendation that it be endorsed.*

The U.S. Senate, however, refused to ratify Article X of the Treaty. This Article guaranteed the land titles of those Mexicans living in Texas who, "due to the unsettled condition" of that State, had not been able to carry out the requirements for possession under Mexican law, such as sowing a crop or building a home. The Mexican government was concerned that striking this article might imperil the land rights of all Mexicans living in the United States. Polk, therefore, sent the highest legal officer in the United States, Attorney General Nathan Clifford, to Mexico together with Senator Ambrose Sevier, chairman of the Foreign Relations Committee. Their mission was to draw up a Protocol "explaining" the Treaty as amended, and to assure Mexico that land grants in territories other than Texas would be protected.

The Texans were determined not to concede the rights of the Mexicans they had defeated to any of their grant lands, with the exception of those Mexicans, like Lorenzo Zavala, who had collaborated with them. In his instructions to Sevier, Polk made that plain: "Neither the President nor the Senate of the United States can ever consent to ratify any Treaty in favor of grantees of land in Texas. Should the Mexican government persist in retaining this article, then all prospect of immediate peace is ended; and of this you may give them an absolute assurance."

Polk then pointed the gun: "Without peace they must be destroyed. . . . You are to insist strenuously upon the ratification of the Treaty by the Mexican Government just as it

---

the hope that Mexican Catholics would believe the Virgin had sanctioned their humiliation and covered it with her mantle.[15]
* Trist's salary was not paid until many years later, and there was some doubt about his official status.

has been ratified by the Senate. Should the war be renewed, the Mexican Government can never again expect to make peace on terms so favorable as those contained in the present Treaty."[16] The Congress of Mexico ratified the Treaty on May 19, 1848, 57 votes to 35, on the theory that it was better to cede half their country than lose it all. This threat also undoubtedly prompted the remaining Mexican states to endorse the ratification in the incredibly short period of two weeks.

The Treaty fixed the new boundaries of the United States, capturing a vast territory that now encompasses the states of New Mexico, Arizona, California, Utah and Nevada, and parts of Colorado, Kansas, Oklahoma, and Wyoming. One of the most important documents the United States has ever signed, it increased the area of the United States by over 50 per cent, gave it excellent ports on the Pacific, provided the nation with prodigious mineral wealth, and guaranteed that this country would achieve dominance in the Western Hemisphere.

It was bitterly resented by the Mexican people. "What used to be called stealing is now called annexation," said a popular government official of the period. It was feared that although the Mexicans living in the conquered territory had been offered U.S. citizenship, they would be looked upon as second-class citizens. There was also fear that the surrender of California to the United States might invite the seizure of Mexico's entire west coast.[17]

So ended the first massive intervention in a foreign country by the forces of the United States. A war for the conquest of land, impelled by the racist theory of Manifest Destiny, it prepared Robert E. Lee, Jefferson Davis, and many others who took part in it to seize arms again in the attempt to perpetuate slavery in their own country 13 years later. Decided by a combination of bribery, treachery, and superior weapons, the war against Mexico ended with a peace treaty signed in fear that the invaders would take the whole country.

GADSDEN'S "PURCHASE"

U.S. DEPREDATIONS on Mexican territory continued for many years after the war was officially ended, and by 1853 the Mexican government had presented claims for damages amounting to ten million dollars. This sum was paid, not in satisfaction of Mexico's claims but in consideration of cession of yet more territory—over 45,000 square miles of land known to be rich in precious minerals (copper, gold and silver) in present-day southern New Mexico and Arizona.*

Railroad promoter James Gadsden, who was then Ambassador to Mexico, negotiated the treaty that bears his name. The Gadsden Purchase provided the roadbed for two continental railroads connecting the east with California. "The US was much the gainer by the terms of this Treaty,"[18] even though Mexico rejected Gadsden's demands for a cession of Baja California and more of Chihuahua and Sonora.

The slaveholders, who were setting policy in the Buchanan administration, still sought new territory for the extension of slavery, and impatiently awaited the signal to fall on Chihuahua, Coahuila and Sonora, hoping by the conquest of the whole of northern Mexico to create a sufficient number of states to give it control of the Senate. In the ensuing period, the U.S. ruling groups continued to display great interest in the mines and fertile fields of Sonora, and in 1858 the President recommended to Congress that the United States should assume a temporary protectorate over Sonora and Chihuahua and that it should establish military posts there.[19] For many years, disputes arose over the boundary of Mexico and the United States. A pure Zapotec Indian, President Benito Juárez, had presented Mexico's claim over land that was separated by the Río Grande from Mexico by a flood in 1864, a

---

* California gold and Nevada silver helped save the Union, but in New Mexico the "gold" turned out to be copper, and today New Mexico is the nation's leading source of uranium.

claim substantiated by an international boundary commission in 1912. Part of the disputed territory—the Chamizal area at El Paso—was not determined finally until 115 years after the original treaty was signed.*

2. Land Grab

As A result of the Mexican War, the United States obtained an area as great as England, Ireland, Scotland, France, Spain, Portugal and Germany together. For the Mexicans living to the north of the new boundaries, the ignominy did not end with the signing of the treaty. For these Mexicans, writes the Mexican author Mario Gill, "the tragedy was more terrible than for those of this side. We lost half our country. They lost it all. And if this were not enough, they still had to endure the presence of the invaders, the destroyers of their nation."[1]

The rights of the new citizens were at least formally guaranteed in the Treaty of Guadalupe Hidalgo. Article IX of the document as ratified by the U.S. Senate clearly stipulates:

"Mexicans in the territories aforesaid . . . shall be incorporated in the Union of the United States and admitted . . . to the enjoyment of all the rights of the citizens of the United States . . . and in the meantime shall be

* For over a century, until Fidel Castro denounced the theft before the world, the U.S. held this valuable piece of El Paso real estate. On October 28, 1967, Tijerina looked on while Mrs. Lyndon Johnson and Señora Díaz Ordaz together snipped a white satin ribbon, marking the new U.S.-Mexico boundary. Said President Ordaz, "More than one hundred years were necessary to obtain a decision on this just claim made by Benito Juarez—to him, we pay homage."[20]

maintained and protected in the free enjoyment of their liberties and property." Since these rights as citizens were guaranteed in the Treaty, the military government should have been terminated. However, the Kearny code of occupation remained in effect in New Mexico, and commandants continued to be appointed from Washington. Moreover, the attitude of the United States toward treaties with Mexico reflected its prevailing judgment of Mexicans. This attitude was that there was very little difference between an Indian and a Mexican; serious and respectful diplomacy was out of place in either case.

Santa Fe, founded in 1609, had been continuously governed from Mexico except for an interval in 1680 when the Pueblo Indians revolted and drove the Spaniards from the province, killing 400 settlers. Twelve years later, a newly appointed governor of New Mexico, Diego de Vargas, returned to make peace with the Pueblos, and established towns that survive to this day.

For almost three centuries groups of settlers from "old" Mexico moved north and unloaded their caravans in the shade of the cottonwoods along the Santa Fe River. They relished the food of the Mexican Indian, the tortilla, beans and chile unknown in Europe, and their Spanish was spiced with words native to Mexico. Until 1823, indeed, they were subjects of Spain, but only an occasional priest or officer had actually seen the mother country across the ocean. Not more than 300,000 Spaniards came to the Americas in the three colonial centuries and many of these, of course, came only for short periods and later returned.

The State of New Mexico is a trifle larger than Poland. The first schools, churches and municipal governments in present-day United States were in New Mexico. At the time of the U.S. invasion about 70,000 Mexican and Indian people lived there, not counting the tribes of semi-nomadic Indians who hunted and fished across its boundaries. The Pueblo Indians—a sedentary, agricultural people who numbered about 40,000—lived in their small compact villages, as they have from pre-historic times to the present.[2]

Under Spanish rule Indians were acknowledged to be the owners of lands they possessed and cultivated. This provision was strengthened by agreements reached with the Pueblos after the return of De Vargas, and the government of Mexico recognized the same right.

THE GRANTS

THE ANCESTORS of today's land grantees made their homes along the river valleys in communal villages, and farmed small strips of land bordering the rivers or streams.

Spanish and Mexican laws of land tenure had provided for assignment of tracts of land not occupied by the sparse Indian population. Colonial Spain offered land to encourage settlement of the northern provinces of Mexico, and after Mexico freed herself from the Spanish crown, grants were made in groups of at least twelve families to soldiers who had distinguished themselves in that revolution. In February 1834, Mexico's Secretary of Relations in regard to colonization of land invited "the robust arms of the Mexican to employment in colonization of those beautiful and fruitful territories (of New Mexico) " with emphasis on the "families of unemployed soldiers of the revolution."

The boundaries of the grants were well defined; a stream, a ridge, and the boundary of an adjacent grant were among the limits most frequently described. A rough map often accompanied the application. The act of taking possession of the land was marked by a legal ceremony participated in by a magistrate and other authorities.

Application for a grant could be made by an individual, but most frequently grants were made to groups of 20 families or more. Each owned his house in the village, and the land he tilled, but the grazing and forest land was held in common for the collective use of the township. The common land amounted to as much as 90 per cent of the grant and could not be sold.

Statutes established self-government of the land grants. Owners or proprietors of a grant "to any colony, community or town, or to any person or persons . . . shall become a body corporate and politic." Each person owning any interest in the grant could vote at the biennial elections.[3] This *ejido* pattern of land tenure followed the system once general in parts of Spain, and still persisting in the Pyrenees.* In the northern counties of New Mexico, the communal form of land ownership provided the stability and mutual protection that enabled it to endure through the centuries. In the early history of New Mexico, there are no accounts of starvation or want. The economy was not a monetary one. A day's work was the usual medium of exchange. "The men exchanged 'days of work' with one another," writes Dr. Horacio Ulibarrí.[5] Following a custom that persists to this day, the ditch association taxed each man so many days of work for a certain number of water rights.

Dr. Margaret Mead, in a study of northern New Mexico, noted: "By the end of the 17th century they had founded many communities such as those they had known in Mexico. Their cultural contacts were with Mexico." She points out that historically and geographically the inhabitants form the fringe of another group, the people of Latin America, whose culture, language and religion they share. "The basic cultural fact of traditional Spanish-American life is the village," states Dr. Mead. "These villages . . . belong to people who depend on one another for their livelihoods and their diversions.

* In Mexico, community control through the *ejido,* a goal of the Zapatistas, is today replacing landlord rule. Nearly half of farm-operating families are village members with rights to *ejido* lands. In today's Mexico, these *ejidos* suffer from economic competition and ideological attack, but "for those who remain without land, becoming an *ejidatario* is seen as a definite improvement in conditions."[4]

. . . Work is an accepted and inevitable part of everyday life. Everyone is expected to do his part. Tools are shared. Cooperation on some occasions involves the whole village."[6]

And as Reies Tijerina stresses, "the ties of our culture with the land are indivisible." The moment the war was over a struggle began to wrest the land from its Mexican owners. The Anglo invaders had found, to their chagrin, that most of the watered land was owned by long-settled Mexican farmers. They now devised diabolical schemes to seize it.

Sam Houston, ex-President of the Texas Republic, brazenly expressed the prevalent opinion that white men had always cheated Indians, "and that since Mexicans are no better than Indians, I see no reason why we should not go on the same course now and take their land."[7]

Stealing land was facilitated by the suppression of the population by military rule, and by the mistaken confidence of many grantees that their right to farms handed down from father to son for generations was unquestioned. Moreover, by a law of 1862, the grantees were required to bear all the expense of investigation and survey, and having little money, they saw no reason to rush into litigation to prove ownership of what everyone knew was theirs.

Unfamiliarity with the U.S. tax system also played a part. Spain and Mexico had taxed the product, but never the land. After 1895, Indo-Hispanos suddenly found their farms being sold for unpaid taxes they had never heard of, the accumulated debt concealed from the owner until the day his land was auctioned to a friend of the sheriff for a few cents an acre.

In violation of the Treaty, moreover, the new government refused to recognize the communal system of land tenure. When the Surveyor General arrived from Washington, he began at once to assign *ejido* lands to the public domain. "Grants of land, even though assured by the Treaty of Guadalupe Hidalgo, passed, through court action or deceit, from the Spanish American to the hands of greedy speculators."[8] Washington sent in a series of Surveyors General, charged with dealing with questions of ownership. These were not necessarily professional surveyors—the job could go to anyone to whom the administration owed a political debt. Irregularities in surveys were profuse.

Surveyor General H. M. Atkinson for one was openly in the cattle business with the notorious Thomas B. Catron, the First National Bank of Santa Fe, and other members of the Santa Fe Ring, which bilked Mexican farmers of thousands of acres. For years the Ring ruled imperiously. "It elected legislators and delegates to Congress. It had the ear of the administration at Washington and could build up and pull down men at its pleasure. Whoever dared to oppose its purposes or methods, was purchased or intimidated into silence, or killed."[9]

The kingpin of the Ring was Catron, a big-time speculator who became the largest landowner in the United States, obtaining possession of more than a million acres, including the famous Tierra Amarilla grant. He served for years as a U.S. Attorney General and was the first U.S. Senator when New Mexico became a state.

Tijerina frequently speaks of the "organized criminal conspiracy" of the Santa Fe Ring. He accuses the United States of complicity in the conspiracy, one element of which was the disappearance of titles proving land ownership. These documents had been burned or sold as "wrapping paper" by Governor Pile in 1870, and it was not until 1960 that some of the records were recovered from a Missouri book dealer, who had bought them from the family of Thomas B. Catron, Attorney General of the Territory at the time they vanished.*

A Court of Private Land Claims was established in 1891, "made up of judges from the South who believed in slavery," states Tijerina. It was deliberately set up to reduce the acreage belonging to native New Mexicans. More than two-

* Bancroft describes the "bulky accumulation of 160 years of land titles" as being "most shamefully neglected under U.S. rule," and refers to the "stupid blunder" by which one half the old Spanish archives were lost in the time of Governer Pile.[10]

thirds of the petitions that came before it were rejected, while many of those confirmed were reduced in size. "Legal-appearing devices were found whereby land grant heirs could be cheated, and by the time it had closed its books in 1904, the Federal Government had acquired control over 52 million acres of land in New Mexico," writes Dr. Frances Swadesh.[11] Nine million acres were set aside for the National Forest. A high percentage of these acres was carved out of grant lands that had been approved by the Court.

Theodore Roosevelt, acting on behalf of the railroad and lumber barons, vigorously advanced the alienation of large areas of communal fields and forests for the Federal Forest Service. The heirs were largely unaware of these transactions that usually took place in far off Washington, and only reacted when fences were erected cutting off their access to grazing and firewood.

Congress reserved for itself the right to pass upon each land claim in New Mexico by direct legislative action. No provisions were made for incorporating traditional concepts of communal land ownership, or for setting up an appeal system from congressional decision. "No claimant could secure congressional affirmation of his title unless he was able to spend a long period of time in Washington, and was abundantly equipped with funds to organize a lobby to smooth the passage of a private act confirming the land claim."[12]

By the end of the Civil War, many land grant villages had become ghost towns, particularly in the eastern part of the state where they were overrun by Texas cattlemen and Confederate soldiers seeking their fortunes. In the north the village economy was ruined by land robbery, and in a single generation the population was reduced from modest self-sustenance to poverty. But the grantees held on, and in the northernmost county of Río Arriba, the grants remained the center of sporadic resistance. The two largest of these are the Tierra Amarilla and the San Joaquín grants, whose families became the backbone of Tijerina's movement.

At the August 1969 trial of Baltazar Martinez, a defendant in the Tierra Amarilla Courthouse case, Dr. Swadesh presented the following figures: "In 1832, more than 580,000 acres belonged to the heirs of the Tierra Amarilla Land Grant. In 1969, the heirs have only 10,000 acres. Under the San Joaquín Grant, the heirs had between 472,000 and 600,000 acres in 1806. In 1969, they have only 1,411 acres."

Just as the biologist places a sample of living tissue under his microscope to study the structure of an entire organism, so we might examine the fate of one of these grants, the San Joaquín del Río de Chama. This grant was made in 1806 to the heads of 39 families, whose descendants today number more than 350 families. They live on a fraction of their original holdings in the villages which are within the grant: Coyote, founded in 1820; and Canjilón, Capulin, and Gallina, founded in 1832.

The Surveyor General approved this grant in 1872. It was submitted to Congress, and the Committee on Public Lands reported out a bill confirming it to the heirs. For years they believed this action confirmed their title. However, Congress did not act on the bill. In Washington, unknown forces intervened, and without the claimants' knowledge it was relegated to the Court of Private Land Claims for further consideration. The Court refused to recognize anything but the small plots on which the homes and cultivated fields were located, and would confirm none of the land held in common. The Federal government finally exercised its domain over the land, turning it over to the Forest Service.

Representative Antonio Fernández of New Mexico later told Congress: "Those poor families appealed to lawyers for help but were without funds to finance an intelligent investigation. They have met with a firm denial of assistance, and were told that this case settled the matter once and for all."[13] On that occasion Fernández asked Congress for an early hearing, complete investigation, and action on behalf of the heirs. But Fernández is dead and Congress has never acted. Most of their land in the hands of the Forest Service, the villagers are now members of Tijerina's Alianza.

As would be expected, a denial of the Mexican people's political rights accompanied the suppression of their property rights. Statehood with its accompanying civil rights was withheld for 66 years—until an Anglo majority could be assured. As late as 1909, President Theodore Roosevelt fought admission of New Mexico to the Union, arguing that its people, having been stifled by their Spanish heritage, were not equal to the rest of the nation in intellect, habits or customs. After taking part in the invasion of Cuba, this booster of rising imperialism appointed two of his Rough Riders to serve as governors of Arizona and New Mexico.[14]

Following the establishment of the Territorial Government in 1852, all Hispano adult males were legally entitled to vote; however, in practice public offices were so monopolized by the dominant Anglos that the New Mexicans (still a majority) "had little voice in the passing of legislation which became increasingly oppressive against the poor,"[15] such as the introduction of imprisonment for debt. Mexican leaders held mass meetings in Santa Fe to demand statehood and oppose slavery, but their petitions were met with sharp rebuke from Washington.

Throughout the period of territorial status, as well as after the granting of statehood to Arizona and New Mexico, the Indo-Hispanos were systematically deprived of the very rights guaranteed in the Treaty of Guadalupe Hidalgo. Therefore, Tijerina regards the struggle to enforce the Treaty and its Protocol as a fundamental issue in the fight for the rights of the Mexican minority. He has accused the United States of ignoring the Treaty, and sought to popularize its provisions.

In an effort to provoke serious official consideration of the question, he has suggested that the document was invalid, since Polk had fired Trist before it was signed and two articles were eliminated by Congress. "Therefore, the United States had no legal right to the Southwest," he announced to a Los

Angeles press conference. "Cuba may be asked to submit the document to the United Nations to determine its validity."[16] Tijerina further argues that if the Treaty is not binding, then "the protocol signed between the United States and Mexico is the only valid document ending the war." For, in stating that the land grants would "preserve the legal value which they possess," the protocol specifically guaranteed that the United States would recognize the grants of lands made by Mexico in the ceded territories.

3. Making of a Leader

REIES LOPEZ TIJERINA was born in Falls City near San Antonio, Texas on September 21, 1923 in an area torn from Mexico by the United States. Although this conquest took place 80 years before his birth, it fixed his place in society as a member of a Mexican minority. His grandfather was nearly lynched by a ruling majority that spoke English.

At an early age he heard accounts of cruelties carried out by Mexican-hating ranchers and Texas Rangers. These ruthless men were determined to keep Mexicans at work in fields where black slaves had once grown the cotton that made the owners rich.

Reies himself became a worker when he was four years old. His father showed him how to pile into a heap the cotton that fell to the ground. This small pile was added to the family pickings.

Things were tough in Texas. Even whole families couldn't make it on 25 or 35 cents an hour. They headed north, to the beet fields of Colorado, Wyoming, or even Michigan. Forget about school. There has always been a double standard of school attendance—one for the children of migrants and one for everybody else. Reies Tijerina did not learn English until he was eleven, to read and write until still later.

In the Spring, the highways north from San Antonio were filled with truckloads of human beings, packed too tight to breathe, 60,000 of them, grandparents, parents, children and even babies. They made the long and difficult trek to the Michigan beetfields that supply our tables with sugar. In six months they might average $500-$600 total pay and to earn this everyone had to work, including little children. Low as these earnings were, they were more than they would have made by staying in Texas and picking cotton.[1]

Every April, they rode north in trucks and sometimes in cattle cars. The Texas ranchers, enraged when agents for the sugarbeet companies began tapping their great reserves of cheap labor, passed a law to bar out-of-state recruiters (Texas Emigrant Agent Law of 1929). But, the law didn't keep the people from leaving and the ranchers were forced to bring in more Mexican workers to pick cotton.

The people of Mexico have always resented the way Mexican labor is treated in Texas, and bitter charges of racial discrimination against those workers appeared in the Mexican press. "We are not the Servants of the Continent," declared an article published in Mexico City during World War II. "The Nazis of Texas are not political partisans of the Fuehrer of Germany nor do they desire his triumph; but indeed they are slaves of the same prejudices and superstitions."[2]

When Tijerina was in his teens, the family spent four years harvesting crops in Michigan, Ohio and Indiana. Neighbors from San Antonio, the Escobars, also made the trip north, and whichever family finished their row first hurried to help the other. Attractive María Escobar later was to become Reies' first wife, travel the country with him, and bear his five older children.

During the depression, Reies and his brothers occasionally worked in factories in Pontiac. But there was ugly discrimination in Michigan, as well as Texas. It was a hard life, and young Reies thought about ways of improving it. One day an evangelist came along, and Reies wondered whether the brotherhood of Christ could provide the solutions he had not found in the beetfields. He was 17 when this itinerant preacher offered him a chance to go to a three-year Assembly of God school near El Paso, Texas. There he is remembered by those who taught him as a "sincere, reform-conscious student and as a fiery and effective preacher with sometimes unorthodox views."[3]

After graduating from Bible School, Tijerina did international evangelistic work on both sides of the Mexican border. "Entering Mexico as an itinerant religious leader, he left it deeply motivated by the philosophy of the Mexican revolution," wrote Dr. Knowlton.[4]

During this period he wrote a book, *¿Habrá Justicia en La Tierra?* (Will There Be Justice on Earth?), but did not seek to have it translated into English or published when he returned to the United States because, "At that time, I believed all Anglos to be the enemy."

In 1955, with 19 families, he established a cooperative village in Arizona called Valley of Peace. They built homes, a school and church, raised and marketed their own cotton.

The growers of Arizona's million-dollar crops, however, saw this effort by former migratory workers as a threat, and drove them out in 1957. "The village was all burned down and we had to leave Arizona. We were invited to come to northern New Mexico. There I learned of the land grants. I inquired and investigated and learned the people's dream. So strong, it was strong enough to move me.

"I felt New Mexico was the only spot in the Southwest where there was a spark of hope for Spanish-Americans—where they could make their rights felt in the eyes of the government."*

* Tijerina's statements are from testimony at the Bernalillo County Courthouse, December 10, 1968.

But more information was needed to prove these rights, and for the next three years Tijerina and his whole family picked cotton to raise funds for his research in Mexico. They saved every penny. "We did not even spare the children money for a pair of socks," he said later.

Between seasons, while he pored over the archives in Mexico City, Reies' wife and children waited in the border city of Juarez, assisted financially by his brothers.

This feeling of kinship, binding the most distant relatives to stand by one another in time of need or danger, is a significant factor that the ruling class has failed to take into account in its efforts to destroy Tijerina and the land grant organization he founded, the Alianza. It is apparent in Tijerina's own family, where his brothers Anselmo, Ramón, and Cristobal have all taken part in Alianza struggles. Active supporters are Reies' children: particularly his oldest son Reies Hugh, known in the family as "David," who says of his father, "he is the only real teacher I have ever had."

Alianza members usually join by family groups, and when one of them appears before a court, the face of the defendant seems to be repeated many times among the spectators. As Dr. Margaret Mead has observed, "To be Spanish-American is to belong to a family."

The Tijerina family next moved to Albuquerque, where Reies broke with his church, maintaining that tithes should go to the poor, not to buy the minister a new car. Some have said that the biblical framework of his speech is a gimmick, others that he is a religious fanatic. Neither is true. Like his dark suit, Tijerina's religious terminology stems from the days of his itinerant evangelism. He spices his rhetoric with biblical references, as did the silver-tongued orators of our grandfather's day, and for the same reason.

Although Tijerina is basically a religious man, he does not attend church nor urge others to seek salvation in prayer. When Reies describes events in biblical terms, it is because these are the allusions most familiar to his listeners. It is a cul-

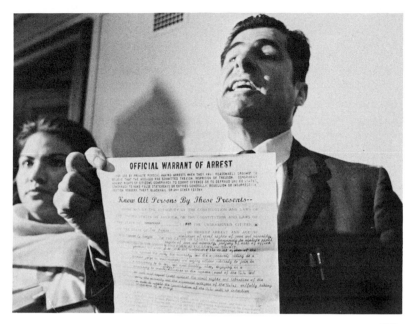

Reies Tijerina at Senate Judiciary Committee, June 1969. He presented a warrant for a Citizen's Arrest of Warren E. Burger, who had been nominated for Chief Justice. Tijerina accused Burger of "conspiracy to violate the civil rights of minorities."

Cristobal and Reies Tijerina outside the Alianza Headquarters

tural, literary expression rather than a religious one. Most of
the Alianza members are at least nominally Catholic. Reies'
former Protestant denomination embodies a militant anti-Ca-
tholicism. So there is no question of what some have called a
"religious rebellion." Tijerina's is a rebellion against impossible conditions of life.

"After considerable research in Washington, after spending
a whole year looking into the archives in Mexico City, after
visiting Spain, and then examining microfilms of the grants in
Albuquerque, I began to learn what had happened to all the
documents," explained Tijerina.

"When I had become satisfied of the accuracy of the facts, I
began daily radio programs [Station KABQ] in Spanish for
two whole years, explaining the historical and legal background, the fraud perpetrated on the grantees, the destruction of records and other crimes against the people.

"The people were totally dependent on this land, physically, morally, spiritually. I saw the land question as the hope
of the Southwest."

Throughout one cold winter, Tijerina talked to the people
of the northern counties, and the first thing he concluded was
that one grant alone could not win. To amass the strength
necessary for the battle to regain the land, it was necessary to
unite all the heirs of all the northern grants. This he did,
through meetings, the radio and by means of a widely distributed newspaper column in the Albuquerque *News Chieftain,*
starting September 7, 1963.

Listening to the painful narrative of cases that had been
thrown out of court by New Mexico judges who often were
landowners themselves, he decided that wider public support
must be created, both by education and by demonstrative actions. The first of these projects was aimed at obtaining the
aid of the Mexican Republic for a petition to the United Nations.

And so 1959 found Tijerina in Mexico with a delegation
representing 107 dispossessed families. Mexican writer Mario

Gill reported at the time that the loss of their grants in New Mexico, "with the connivance of venal judges and the indifference of Washington authorities," had caused Mexican-Americans to seek help from the government of Mexico. "From among them there has arisen a leader, a sort of apostle of the cause of Mexican-Americans, the symbolic man in whom the ideals of a people are embodied—the Mexican people oppressed in the US."[5]

"Dedicated to the task of raising a wave of solidarity among his racial brothers," Tijerina and the delegation were in Mexico to turn over to President Lopez Mateos a memorial signed by thousands of Mexican-Americans. It asked that the Mexican government intervene with Washington to demand the fulfillment of the Treaty of Guadalupe Hidalgo, and adherence to the Universal Declaration of Human Rights, "which is today being violated to the injury of the Mexican residents of the Southwestern States of the United States."

The people of Mexico received their brothers warmly, but their government did not challenge U.S. violations of the Treaty. On two subsequent occasions the grantees sought to renew their mission to Mexico, but both attempts failed. In the spring of 1964, the Alianza planned a motorcade from Albuquerque to Mexico City, but Tijerina was arrested when he went to Chihuahua to map the route of the caravan. "The shock and anger which this abrupt and unexplained action aroused throughout Mexico, where festivities for the New Mexico pilgrims were being planned, was reflected in news reports."[6]

Again in 1967 plans to visit Mexico were frustrated when the FBI threatened to arrest a motorcade of delegates if it should attempt to cross the border.

When Reies Tijerina began to unite the heirs to land grants, slander and rumor were widely spread concerning their intentions. Therefore, although the most forceful expression of Tijerina's ideas has always been in speech, he found it necessary to issue a pamphlet summarizing the Alianza position. It was printed in Spanish and English, and distributed throughout the State.[7]

He began by presenting the legal basis for claims to the *pueblos* (villages) that originated in Spanish law, were affirmed by the Treaty of Guadalupe Hidalgo and upheld by the Constitutions of New Mexico and the United States.

From a delineation of these rights, Tijerina drew political, legal and judical conclusions concerning the privileges vested in the heirs to the grants. The booklet described the Alianza's attitude toward the courts, and forecast the tactics that were to determine the Alianza's actions in the three years that followed.

Tijerina opened with a reminder that more than a century had passed since the United States invaded and occupied New Mexico, "yet the question of the land grants, far from being resolved, has sunk into a morass of fraud, forgery and perjury."

After quoting from the Treaty, drawn up to protect property rights in New Mexico, Tijerina cited those sections of the U.S. and State constitutions that forbid depriving any person of property without due process or just compensation.

Next he went to the heart of today's struggle: "None of these grant lands and waters which the United States asserts it acquired from Mexico under the Treaty . . . ever formed any part of the *public domain*. These lands and waters cannot be taken for any purpose."

Then, in a forewarning ignored by the authorities, he declared:

"There are many trespassers on these Land Grants who have through various and devious means seized these lands both contrary to law and the true owner's interest. The true owners of these lands have the legal right to use all the force necessary to oust these trespassers."

In a further chapter, Tijerina explained that the majority of these grants were to *pueblos*, that is, to villages. A *pueblo* had a political jurisdiction, being governed by six or twelve councilmen, according to size. It had a judicial existence, and in addition was allowed to own property.

He quoted an 1859 decree of the first Surveyor General: "the existence of a town when the United States took possession of the country being proven, it is to be taken as evidence of a grant to said town, and when recognized as a town by the Mexican Government, it is believed to be a good and valid grant, *and the land claimed severed from the public domain.*"

"Consequently," wrote Tijerina, "the villages have the legal right to use all the force necessary and all the police power necessary to insure their constituents the peaceful enjoyment of their rights."

The pamphlet ends with an appeal to Anglos: "The Indo-Hispano people of New Mexico are no longer a disunited people, but are uniting for the first time to recover and preserve their birthright and cultural heritage . . . each day they are getting stronger and have more confidence in themselves.

"The just cause of the Indo-Hispano people is their struggle to restore authority vested in the community, the natural unit of society, and down with all Anglo anarchists."

4. Enemy in the Forest

IN FEBRUARY of 1963 the Alianza was born. "The object of the Alianza," Tijerina said, "was to give the Indo-Hispanic people of the Southwest pride in their heritage, and force the Anglo to respect him, just like we respect them."

The full name of the new organization was "Alianza Federal de Mercedes"—Federated Alliance of Land Grants—and the first convention, held in September of that year, was attended by more than 800 delegates representing 48 New Mexico land grants.

Of over 50 land grants in the state, the Alianza resolved to concentrate on two, the Tierra Amarilla and the San Joaquín del Río Chama, both in Río Arriba County. Later, activity was also developed around two smaller grants, Piedra Lumbre adjacent to San Joaquín, and the Los Trigos Grant in San Miguel County.

At the convention, the main discussion centered around plans to pool the efforts of the assembled grantees. They would hire attorneys and bring political pressure to bear on Washington. A highlight of the convention was a report on Reies Tijerina's trip to Washington, recently made to enlist the aid of the Attorney General on the land-grant issue. On the same trip, Tijerina had attended the American Emancipation Centennial in Chicago and invited its Negro president, Dr. Alton Davis, to be keynote speaker at the Alianza convention. Mexico's former president, Miguel Alemán, had been a speaker at the centennial and expressed interest in the land-grant struggle.[1]

Alianza membership increased rapidly in the following years, due to an influx of villagers angered by what appeared to them to be harsh, unfair and capricious decisions by the National Forest Service that were forcing many of them to migrate.[2]

The Forest Service determines the number of animals that may be grazed in a specific area.* In 1965, in a deliberate effort to oust the small farmers, their grazing permits were reduced by 45 per cent. "Such measures hit the 50,000 northern Spanish-Americans where it hurts, in the stomach as well as the heart," wrote a Santa Fe reporter.[3]

By 1967 more than 20,000 were forced to leave their ham-

---

* For lush grasslands, it might be one cow a month for each 1½ acres. For poor scrub timber land, it might take 20 acres to sustain a cow for one month.

lets for temporary work as migrants—some going as far as Wisconsin to can tomatoes and cucumbers.

While logging firms contracted with the Forest Service for immense areas on their ancestral land, the grantees were forbidden to cut stovewood without a permit. Moreover, the men had lost their jobs at the locally run lumber mill because it was unable to compete with the larger outfits, which hired out-of-county help.

Hatred of the *rinche,* the Forest Ranger, was increasing. Separated by language and social outlook from the local population, the Ranger often assumed the arrogant stance of a member of an army of occupation toward recalcitrant natives.

Of ten million acres of National Forest land in the state, nearly a million were taken from communal grant lands which had already been confirmed by the courts. In the northern counties, the U.S. Forest Service is today the biggest landowner—60 per cent is now in federal hands. "The establishment of the National Forest System in New Mexico alienated millions of acres from the village ejidos without compensation."[4]

The theft continues. Tobias Leyba of Canjilón points in the distance to the former boundaries of the village pasture. "Now, look what they've left us," he says, indicating the Forest Service fence a few feet from his front porch. "This is why I'm with the Alianza." For Mr. Leyba's eleven children, a milk cow is a barrier against hunger.

"A cold war has come into existence between the villagers and the Forest Service," Dr. Knowlton warned. "They believe that they are being deliberately squeezed out of the National Forests to make room for larger Anglo-American cattle and sheep outfits."

It may seem strange that the villager of the north should consider the Forest Ranger to be his ever present enemy, hemming him in and depriving his family of food and fuel. The image of the Forest Service created by a high-powered public relations campaign is that of "A romantic figure of the

West . . . a lone rider of the mountains and guardian of the Forests," to quote an example from the stream of self-laudatory publications that pours forth from Washington.

The facts are far from "romantic." The Forest Service is an army of men, 11,000 strong, with 16,000 seasonal employees, whose chief is appointed by the Secretary of Agriculture. It includes a hierarchy of executives whose function is to administer 186 million acres of land—eight per cent of the area of the entire nation. It commands one-quarter of the total land area of the eleven western states, yielding invaluable forest and mineral products.

In volume of timber sales alone, it is a big business. Over 30,000 individual sales of timber are made each year, with a total value that exceeds 200 million dollars. Proceeds go to the U.S. Treasury. The local Forester has complete authority to negotiate these contracts. "Some are inclined to foster large sales to large companies, whether local or not, to simplify problems of policing the terms of the contracts."[5]

Far exceeding timber sales are mineral prospecting and development on national forest lands. Nationwide, close to 10,000 leases are in force. In the final hours of his administration, former Secretary of the Interior Stewart L. Udall called for a complete overhaul of the nation's antiquated mineral-leasing law as a means of curbing "an outright giveaway of vital natural resources."[6]

In New Mexico, most of these leases are to out-of-state corporations, at a great loss to the local population. The wealth and variety of New Mexico's mineral deposits are enormous, and their value increases daily; in 1968 the state's mineral production approached a billion dollars.[7]

Efforts to force mining companies to pay their share of severance and excise taxes are made each legislative session, but state administrations tied directly to big business won't act. Subsidies and bonuses to new arrivals in the State have been the order of the day.

Kerr McGee, incorporated in Delaware and part of the Morgan group, is one of several giants that have acquired leases on federal lands. It has extended its activities from Nigeria, Angola, Canada and Venezuela to "colonial" New Mexico, where it holds close to 28,000 acres for the extraction of gas, oil and nuclear fuels, and is pursuing an aggressive program for discovery of uranium deposits.

Kennecott, another member of the Morgan group, in 1968 alone sent close to a hundred thousand tons of copper to its Baltimore refinery from New Mexico, adding the precious ore to what it had stolen from the Chilean people. It is also digging in the land grant area along the Río Arriba-Táos County line for rare metals used, among other things, to coat rocket nozzles.

Phelps Dodge not only extracts valuable minerals from Peru, Zambia and Puerto Rico but has developed a $110-million plant in New Mexico to tear out irreplaceable copper, leaving behind nothing but a big hole. In this water-scarce section, it has somehow acquired rights to the entire flow of the Gila River.[8]

The Forest Service also provides big business with 55,000 "special use" permits that cover more than three million acres and a wide variety of enterprises. Private concerns are permitted to build and operate hotels, boat docks, and ski lifts in forest preserves, not to mention sawmills, pipelines and roads for the benefit of large corporations.

The Forest Service is evidence of the colonial policy of the Federal government toward the entire West. There are large forests in New York State, for example, but no National Forests. Through this Service, resources of the West are exploited by Washington, D.C. and its friends.

Morris Garnsey, University of Colorado economist, wrote: "the federal government is an absentee landlord in the West. It owns some 275 million acres, nearly 50 per cent of the area of the Mountain States, in national forests, parks and mineral

reserves. The fact that the federal government pays no taxes
on these lands is a constant source of irritation to state and
local governments. Through a policy of getting control of raw
materials, the region becomes a colonial dependency of an industrial empire."[9]

To intensify the grievance of the former owners, federal
control has not prevented serious damage to the land. Huge
tracts of exhausted land testify to the butchery practiced by
get-rich-quick newcomers. For settlers in an arid country,
such methods would have meant suicide. From the Indians
they learned the techniques of irrigation, and the numerous
little mountain valleys, with their fields still green and fertile
after centuries of use, are eloquent witnesses to the fact that
neither the Spaniards, the Mexicans nor the Indians were
ever "land butchers"—of necessity, all were eminent conserva-
tionists.[10]

The conflict is intensified by the methods of the Forest
Service. It operates almost as a law unto itself, unresponsive
to the people of the communities it is supposed to serve. In
his revealing study of the behavior of the Forest Ranger,
Kaufman quotes a letter from the former head of the Bureau
of Land Management: "Many Forest Service men will fight
for a certain course of action and against others, almost without regard to . . . public criticism and opposition."

In a description that could equally well fit the FBI or the
Marines, Kaufman says of the Ranger: "His experiences and
his environment gradually infuse into him . . . a militant
and corporate spirit, with a fierce pride in the Service."[11]

Throughout the West, the Forest Service is accused of dis-
criminating in favor of large owners. In New Mexico, their
"preference for large, corporate leasers as against small stock-
raisers has all but shut Hispano stockmen out from their ancestral rangelands."[12]

Justice William O. Douglas has criticised the management
of national forests, which he says is left to Federal agencies

that promulgate regulations governing the use of these prop-
erties, "but seldom allow a public voice to be heard against
any plan of the agency."[13]

In New Mexico, the Rangers run true to form. At a border
conference held in El Paso in the fall of 1967, Reies Tijerina
told Secretary of Agriculture Freeman that the Forest Service
discriminatcd against Spanish-speaking people in their graz-
ing-permit policies. The Secretary promised an investigation.
Two months later, no investigation had been ordered, and
when reminded, Freeman said he had discussed the charges
with the Forest Service chief and been convinced that "their
policy is fair enough."[14]

An act of Congress in 1891 gave power to establish forest
reserves for the public domain. This power was not used for
the stated purpose of preserving natural resources. Instead,
Forest Service policies were largely responsible for the hated
timber monopoly that ravaged the forests of the West. Big interests such as those of Lumber Baron Frederick Weyerhaeuser and Railroad Magnate J. J. Hill were among the most
prominent influences in the program of "conservation."

In this period extensive depredations of the public timber
were carried on by the railroads, in some cases relying on the
unsurveyed land grants and often with no pretense of legality.
Large quantities of timber in New Mexico were cut from the
public lands by the Santa Fe railroad, and transported out of
the territory, contrary to law.

Recently, Senators Dale McGee of Wyoming and Frank
Church of Idaho called hearings, where scores of opponents
of Forest Service logging practices descended on the Capitol
to protest what they saw as destruction of National Forests sim-
ply to benefit the lumber industry. Speaking in defense of the
Forest Service, representatives of the Weyerhaeuser Company
and the American Plywood Association defended the practice
of "clear-cutting," where trees were leveled like the reaping of
a wheat field. After the hearings, Senator McGee demanded a

two-year moratorium on timber cutting by the Forest Service, which he said had left great forests "depleted to the point that would shame Paul Bunyan."[15]

Hostility to the National Forests began long before New Mexico became a state, and was generated by the Lacey Bill of 1906, which included agricultural lands in the forest reserves. A Colorado congressman attacked the bill because "it left the Secretary of Agriculture with too much discretion in regard to the opening of agricultural lands," and Representative Smith of California secured the exclusion of his state from provisions of the bill, because it was "no part of a proper forest reserve policy" to control range land.[16]

The Forest Service was accused of atrocities—miners had been shot for refusing to vacate ground from which they had been ordered by a Forest Ranger. These, Senator Heyburn of Idaho declared, were "merely illustrations of the manner of administration."

This "manner of administration" again asserted itself at Coyote in August 1969, when James Evans, Forest Service investigator, pointed a gun at Reies Tijerina's head, endangering the lives of his two-year old daughter and over a hundred Alianzistas.

Even the Service function personified by "Smokey the Bear," protecting forests from fire, is questioned by many. By refusing farmers the right to graze, the Forest Service has increased the fire hazard. Grasses allowed to grow year after year form a mat through which fire, under a wind, runs with great rapidity.

It is in limiting grazing land that the Service most often comes into collision with the Indo-Hispanic farmer. The Rangers make unilateral decisions as to the number of grazing permits they will issue and the fees to be charged.

"The Forest Service has consistently been reducing grazing rights and slowly causing the total economic decline of the communities of Northern New Mexico," said Tomás Atencio of the Migrant Council, "only to open the Forest to private outside investors for recreation purposes." They insult the farmers by declaring that cows overgraze the range, and that horses should be raised instead to provide recreation for the tourists. "But," Mr. Atencio observed, "one horse eats as much as two cows, and a cow they can eat, a horse they cannot."[17]

Land grant heirs must pay fines when their cows wander into the 1.4 million acre Carson National Forest, onto land that was lately theirs. If they cannot pay, the Service sells the cows and keeps the money. "Animals not sold will be destroyed," said a Standard Forest Service Form given to farmers in the San Joaquín land grant.[18]

Tijerina has charged that Forest Service Chief Investigator Evans was brought into the area to drive the people off what land they have left. Since coming to New Mexico, Evans has led in the effort to decapitate the Alianza. Brandishing weapons at every confrontation, then declaring that a "potentially violent situation" exists, he is one of those who have succeeded in converting the Alianza's peaceful struggles into a series of criminal prosecutions of Reies Tijerina.

In the years before the Alianza was founded, resistance to Anglo encroachment was kept up by secret organizations such as the Gorras Blancas (White Caps), east of Santa Fe, and the Mano Negra (Black Hand) in Río Arriba County. They engaged in acts of desperation—fence cutting, burning haystacks and sometimes houses. Tijerina, on the contrary, built the Alianza by education of the public, stressing peaceful mass action. The structure of the organization provided for a ruling "cosmic table" of representatives of the various land grants, that passed on all major decisions. Tijerina, not being an heir, had no vote on this body. His leadership was exercised through membership meetings and conventions, that involved everyone supporting the fight for first-class citizenship.

Attendance at mass meetings sometimes reached a thousand —a significant portion of the state's population which is barely one million. Although most of the 300,000 Spanish-speaking people in New Mexico are land grant heirs, as well as their thousands of relatives in other states, not all belong to the Alianza. The press repeatedly placed the number of actual members at 50,000, the purpose of this overstatement being to accuse Tijerina of amassing a fortune from the one dollar monthly dues, which were actually one dollar a month per *family*.

The organization was maintained by donations from individuals, collections at meetings, and proceeds of meals served at the hall. Tijerina helped serve food to the crowd, working quickly as he hailed friends in the waiting line.

No one drew a regular salary—"Hired leaders are like hired gunslingers," said Tijerina, "they work for the side that pays most." The Alianza provided his living quarters, but expenses for trips were debated and voted on by the elders, and often raised at a rally called for the purpose.

Tijerina's habit was to consult everyone around him, vigorously and enthusiastically discuss a budding idea, consider challenges and arguments against it. Once a course of action was fixed, he threw great quantities of energy into carrying it out—on the phone late at night, starting trips by daybreak, pulling young and old into a swirl of activity: a man used to hard work who had found something worth working for.

5. *Language and Culture*

THE HOME of the Alianza in Albuquerque is a two-story, concrete-block building, originally used as a frozen food-packing plant. Its owner had traded the sprawling structure for Tijerina's share of land on the ill-fated Arizona cooperative, plus a monthly sum not always raised.

Rcies Tijerina and his second wife, Patsy, lived upstairs

with their two little children. Various male members of his family and of the organization slept in the basement. Efforts by Alianzistas to improve the cavernous interior were constantly under way, and later when the building became an object of bombings, the construction extended to blocking in the windows.

English was seldom spoken at the Alianza, and when the building resounded with the music of a dance, the tune was either a New Mexico folk melody or a popular Mexican song, interspersed with rock-and-roll as an occasional concession to the youth.

For the tie that bound all Alianza members together was the fight to preserve their culture. Their right to speak Spanish was fiercely defended in spite of opposition from the dominant class that controls the schools and newspapers and tries to eliminate speaking Spanish on the job.

Since the early days of the State, the Spanish language has been fought for. When the New Mexico Constitution was drawn up in 1910, guarantees of Mexican-American civil and political rights were written into it, because their leaders insisted on them and because Anglo representatives of mining, railroad and commercial interests needed Indo-Hispano support to achieve their own goals.

One half of the 70 Republican delegates to the 100-member convention were Indo-Hispano. "They formed a comparatively solid block welded by a common interest . . . the preservation of their traditional way of life and the language of their forefathers."[1]

Against the Enabling Act of 1910, through which President Taft demanded as a condition for statehood that ability to read and speak English be a qualification for holding office, the New Mexicans counterposed the Treaty of Guadalupe Hidalgo. They wrote two unprecedented clauses into their Constitution, the first providing that: "The right of any citizen of the state to vote, hold office or sit upon juries, shall never be restricted . . . on account of religion, race, language or color, or inability to speak, read, or write the English or Spanish languages."

And in order to make it practically impossible to take away this right, the article made a vote of three-fourths of the electors necessary for its amendment, with a further requirement that at least two-thirds of those voting in each county of the State shall vote for such amendment (Article 7, Section 2).

The second article obliged the legislature to provide for the training of teachers "so that they may become proficient in both English and Spanish, to qualify them to teach Spanish-speaking pupils," and followed with the provision that "children of Spanish descent shall never be denied the right and privilege of admission and attendance in the public schools . . . and shall never be classed in separate schools."

The first part of this Article of the Constitution was ignored until Tijerina revived and popularized it. It has yet to be put into force. The second clause, however, prevented a completely segregated school system from arising such as in Texas, where until 1954 three separate schools were the rule in districts with Black, Chicano and white students.

The Alianza's fight against the forced imposition of English won sympathy from the entire Spanish-speaking world, and procured for Tijerina considerable publicity when he went to Spain in 1966. In spite of being ruled by a fascist dictatorship, Spain maintains ties with all the countries of Latin America, including socialist Cuba. Sent there by the Alianza in order to pursue the facts about the grants to their source, he was interviewed in ABC (May 7, 1966) by a Seville newspaperman, Antonio Burgos.

Burgos described Reies Tijerina as "a man of 39 years, self-educated, who speaks perfect Castilian . . . a knight crusading for the rights of Hispanos in the Southwest of the United States, much as Rev. Martin Luther King might be of the aspirations of Black North Americans"

Tijerina was in Seville preparing documentation which the Alianza intended to present to the U.S. Supreme Court,

Burgos explained. "The lands populated by the Spanish explorers, who left behind, together with their language, the singular legacy of *mestizaje*,* became in 1821 a Mexican province. And New Mexico was Mexican until 1846."

"The government of Mexico respected our rights," Tijerina told him, "but the United States dispossessed us. Fifty thousand hectares† of pasture were stolen. In addition they kept us in a state of second-class citizenship, without representation or vote, until 1912."

Burgos then asked: "Does Spanish culture still exist in the southern states of North America?"

"Our culture is Spanish. We want to speak Spanish. But the Anglos press for this cultural legacy to be abandoned—lost," Tijerina answered. "Little children who dare to speak Spanish are run out of school. Everything is English. We are not free to express ourselves in our own language." Referring to New Mexico, Reies added, "Outside of the big cities purely Spanish is spoken. Fifteen percent of the rural population cannot speak English."

"Suppose the Alianza should win its case from the government at Washington?" asked Burgos.

"Then we would build schools where Spanish may once more be taught, we will once more organize the cultivation of the common lands, some of which are rich in minerals. For example, one single *ejido* that now belongs to an Anglo who lives elsewhere yielded him six million dollars worth of uranium."

When Tijerina returned from Spain he brought with him three large volumes containing the laws decreed by Spanish monarchs in their capacity as rulers of the Indies. This code governed a large part of the Western Hemisphere for well over 300 years—from 1492 to 1821. Tijerina made a detailed study of these tomes. They were prominently displayed in the Alianza office and often quoted. One of these decrees, "the

---

* Part Spanish and part Indian ancestry.
† A hectare is approximately 2.5 acres.

first civil rights law in the Americas," as Tijerina called it, was proclaimed in 1573. It established absolute equality of the offspring of Spaniards and Indians. With this edict, says Reies, a *new race* was founded, the Indo-Hispano, to which most of the people of northern New Mexico belong.

Today, many Alianza members proudly mention that they have an Indian grandma or grandpa. It proves that one "belongs" in the area, is a "true native" of the region. Of himself, Tijerina says, "I come from the Tejas tribe: big nose, tall, red skin."

THE FOURTH OF JULY WAS NO PICNIC

THE ALIANZA held its first mass action the weekend of July 4, 1966. For Tijerina, years of striving to share the results of his research were bearing fruit. Now, together with several hundred Alianzistas, he was on his way to petition New Mexico's governor, Jack Campbell.

They started out in Albuquerque early Saturday, July 2 and trudged for three days in 100-degree heat to the capital at Santa Fe. Holiday weekend drivers slowed on the steep hills to read signs that demanded not only return of the land, but first-class citizenship too. "US Movie Industry Slanders Spanish and Indian-Americans," read a placard carried the 62 miles by a young woman. The procession was led by bearded José Luis Sanchez of Albuquerque, who rode a burro, waving the flag of the Tierra Amarilla grant.

"For the first time in history, we're doing this in a united way," Tijerina told the press. "Today, politicians won't listen until the people come out with something spectacular."[2]

When they reached Santa Fe, the marchers found the Governor had gone to California, having detailed Frank McGuire, Director of the Office of Economic Opportunity, to face them. But Tijerina told McGuire that they had not come seeking charity but to present the Governor with their demand for land and full civil rights guaranteed in the Treaty with Mexico, and the Alianzistas voted to wait for him. Camped in a vacant lot on Santa Fe's main artery, they attracted attention. Several carloads drove by to jeer at their banners. Mrs. Gallegos, mother of a large family, was indignant.

"They rode past our camp last night shooting into the air," she said, "and they called out, 'Wet-backs,* go home.' But it is we who belong here, and they who should go home if they don't like it, because we were farming this land when they got here from across the sea."

A vigorous middle-aged farmer, reduced to eking out a meager living from less than ten acres, spoke up. "We will occupy the State Capitol buildings if necessary," he declared. "We will not be bought off. If they offer us money it might help us or our children. But we are fighting for our grandchildren and great-grandchildren who have a right to the land granted our families."

They waited all week, and leaning over the backs of pickups or crowded around a borrowed picnic table, talked to visitors and curiosity-seekers. They had time for long discussions, and to the surprise of those who had taken the jingoistic "patriotism" of some Mexican-American politicians as typical of the whole people, emerged as the most outspoken anti-war group in the State. Some compared the war in Vietnam to the aggression against Mexico, and argued about what kinds of minerals the United States was after in that distant country. All were agreed in denouncing the disproportionate number of Mexican youth drafted and killed.

As a result of the attention they attracted, facts on the land struggle began to appear in the State's newspapers. One article described the methods by which an avaricious rancher seeking land might gain control of it, "with full right to throw the previous owner off."

* Derogatory term used against Mexicans which implies they entered the United States illegally by fording the Río Grande.

"Several famous murders, range wars, and other squabbles
(sic) erupted from such activities toward the close of the last
century in New Mexico. Yesterday's marchers, however, had
more on their minds than repossession of Spanish land grants
taken away from their grandfathers. A common theme among
the marchers was protest against the war in Vietnam. Many
held signs and expressed opinions to the effect that minority
groups are sent to Vietnam to 'fight the white man's war.' "
Paul Vigil, of Bueyeros in Harding County, argued, "I'd
rather be on the side of the Viet Cong than with those ranchers in Harding and Union counties." Vigil asserted that a
Texas-born rancher told him, "You've had it, because you're
not white."[3]

Another reporter commented: "The U.S. Courts have
many times ruled against attempts by heirs to old land grants
to reassert their claims. Tijerina blames this consistent attitude on racial discrimination. He asserts that Spanish Americans have been discriminated against for more than a century
in New Mexico and that they have been consistently squeezed
out of the land holdings and livelihood."

Governor Campbell eventually received the marchers on
July 11. He promised to investigate this "thorny matter" and
personally send the results of his study to President Johnson.
Campbell also finally agreed to ask Johnson for an investigation to be conducted at the executive level. When Campbell
protested that the executive had no authority to settle such issues, Tijerina countered, "the Constitution requires the executive to see that the laws are enforced."

Furthermore, Tijerina said, New Mexico Senator Joseph
Montoya had once offered to introduce a bill in Congress creating a commission to investigate land grant claims, and Representatives Henry Gonzalez of Texas and Edward Roybal of
California agreed to support Montoya's proposal, "but they
didn't feel the time is right yet."

The President's intervention was necessary, Tijerina told
the Governor, because the Claims Court set up by Congress

to settle land disputes in 1891 did not adjudicate the cases fairly, as the people had no proper legal representation. "There were no Spanish-American lawyers in the state at that time." Immediately after the confrontation with the Governor, Tijerina called a meeting of the marchers and a crowd who had joined them. He spoke in Spanish, reviewing the grievances that had brought them from all over New Mexico and from California and Colorado. "Over 60 per cent of our people," he said, "are chained to the pink card of public welfare and powdered milk, because their land has been taken from them. I suppose we should be grateful that they keep us alive with food handouts while they steal our heritage, but we must remember that they feed us only so that when we are needed to fight their wars they can strike up a military band and say 'Come on, Martinez, into the army.'

"Our children go to school and what do they teach them? That we are born of Spanish and Indian blood? [Crowd: 'No!'] Our great mountains, rivers and cities carry Spanish names. Do they tell our children why? ['No!']"

"They commit their greatest crime when they try to take away the language our fathers left us: 'Shut up, don't speak Spanish!' they yell. Real justice has no language. The Treaty of Guadalupe Hidalgo did not say that we must speak English. The Constitution of the United States nowhere says that we must speak English. We will protect our language and our land, not with pistols but with the law.

"Reports of this meeting will be heard from Texas to California. The whole world will know that our stepmother [the U.S. government] has us on bread and water. For justice has no frontier. Justice has no language.

"When the great day comes, when we have won this fight, we will have a great burning. Of Anglos' homes, as they fear? No. Of pink [welfare] cards. When that great day comes, when the Mexican-American has awakened, we will end poverty and the shameful stain of powdered milk."

6. *The Resounding Echo*

THE ECHO Amphitheater is a formation of weather-eroded red sandstone, lying just west of U.S. Route 84, which leads north from Santa Fe to Colorado. The feature that gives the place its name is a cliff facing east, toward the highway, whose face has been worn to a concave shape, like a shallow bowl standing on edge—the bowl being perhaps 500 feet across. The ground approaching the base of the cliff slopes downward to it from three sides, and in this area a campground with picnic shelters, fireplaces and the like has been fitted out by the Forest Service. Thus, the campers occupy the "pit" of the theater, with the echoing hollow cliff in the position of the "band shell."

"REPUBLIC OF SAN JOAQUIN"

THIS WAS the stage where the Alianza in October 1966 chose to present in dramatic style the claim of numerous heirs to the land grant of San Joaquín del Río de Chama. The plan was to physically occupy a part of the grant, and to force the U.S. government, if it wished to end the occupation, to submit to legal proof the proper ownership of the land.

The grant was originally made to Francisco Salazar and a group of settlers, and after the U.S. invasion was approved by Surveyor General Proudfit. In a letter to the Secretary of the Interior, (February 14, 1873), Proudfit had written: "It is now claimed and occupied by hundreds of the descendants of the original grantees, and said grantees have possessed it ever since the grant was made in 1806."

The Forest Service attempted to deny the existence of the

grant in a public statement soon after the Alianza occupied the campground. In the Forest Service version, the only Cañon de Chama "grant" was one of 1,422 acres, which is now under private ownership, surrounded by Carson National Forest. The Alianza occupation of the Echo Amphitheater campground took place in two successive weekends, beginning Saturday, October 15, 1966. The members left the campground during the following week, and it was used normally by tourists until Friday, October 21, when 350 Alianza people returned. Two carloads of FBI agents stationed themselves to watch.

That Friday the campground twinkled with a score of fires in the crisp fall night. The sign by the highway, announcing the Echo Amphitheater campground of the Carson National Forest, was covered with one proclaiming the Republic of San Joaquín del Río de Chama. The gate was emblazoned with slogans: "The US is violating the UN Charter! Down with Land Grabbers! Down with Treaty Violators! US Violates International Law!"

A chain was stretched across the entrance to the campground and a guard posted there. Many travelers continued to stop, their interest excited by the new signs, but no one was admitted except on Alianza business.

The mayor of the pueblo of San Joaquín was Lorenzo Salazar of Coyote, a direct descendant of the Francisco Salazar who had been leader of the original settlers. The new "settlers" unanimously chose the elderly Mr. Salazar as the representative of the heirs to the grant. It was noticeable that in succeeding events, the Federal officials would take no action against Mr. Salazar, or against any heir to the Chama grant, although several were prominent in the happenings at the camp.

On Saturday, October 22, the collision with the Forest Service men occurred, which led to the imprisonment for two years of Reies Tijerina and shorter terms for four others. A party of about 25 Forest Service men, including Special

Hoteville, Arizona Hopi Reservation. Reies Tijerina (*second row, center*); Dan Katchongva, chief of the village (*on Tijerina's right*); Santiago Anaya, vice president of Alianza (*on Tijerina's left*); Cristobal Tijerina (*third row, center*); Jerry Noll (*second row, extreme left*); David Monogye, leader of the traditional Hopis (*first row, extreme left*).

Karl Kernberger

Land grant meeting in Río Arriba County. Alianza Vice President Anaya is on the platform.

Investigator Evans, came to the campground accompanied by several state policemen. Three of the Forest Service men who entered the grounds were detained, along with two of their vehicles. Tijerina stood nearby and watched while the people expressed their pent up resentment.

At the trial, Forester Walt Taylor and District Ranger Phil Smith, both of whom had long records of conflict with the villagers, said they were surrounded by women. "They began to grab at me and tear my clothes," Taylor testified. "Women were dancing around and shouting 'Get him!' " The same episode was described by a witness for the Alianza, Mrs. Isabel García of Albuquerque. Mrs. García said she had been one of the women referred to by Taylor as "dancing around and shouting." She said that the feeling of the people at the confrontation with the Forest Service was, "Now it is our turn."

The third Ranger, Benavidez Zamora, who usually worked in the Cibola Forest across the state, testified that "two ladies saw me, and cried in Spanish, 'There's another one.' But when they heard I could speak Spanish they said, 'He's one of us, don't touch him.' "

Defendants Alfonso Chavez and Ezequiel Dominguez were wearing the badges of peace officers, having been deputized for that duty by Lorenzo Salazar, the mayor. Their part, they said, was to rush in and separate the crowd from the Forest Service men when the latter appeared to be in danger.

Next, Taylor and Smith were taken before a "court" being held at a picnic table by Jerry Noll, an Anglo hanger-on of the Alianza. Noll gave the men "suspended sentences for trespassing," after which they were released.

All witnesses at the trial were in agreement that the "converted" Forest Service trucks were not taken from the campground by the defendants.

Over a hundred members of Alianza families were still at the campground on Wednesday, October 26, when U.S. District Court Judge H. Vearle Payne issued a restraining order. It forbade the campers to perform any acts in the campground not permitted to the general public. One such act, of course, was to be in the campground at all without paying a fee of a dollar a day per vehicle. When this order was served on the campers, Reies' oldest brother, Anselmo Tijerina, was in charge at the Echo Amphitheater. He advised the remaining campers to pack up and leave, and the symbolic territory of the Republic of San Joaquin was vacated within a few hours.

On the same day, FBI agents arrested Reies Tijerina and four others on charges resulting from the clash the preceding Saturday. They were charged with assault on the two Forest Service employees, and with conversion of government property, namely, the two Forest Service pickups the Rangers had been allowed to take with them. With Reies, those arrested were his brother Cristobal, Jerry Noll, Alfonso Chavez, and Ezequiel Dominguez.

At a hearing the following week, Tijerina told a reporter, "We got exactly what we wanted. For the first time, the U.S. government will have to try to prove something it cannot prove."

"Where do you go from here?" he was asked.

"Up." He said the Alianza intention was to "reach the Supreme Court."

Other stirring events, notably the one at Tierra Amarilla, were to take place before the five came to trial in November 1967 in the U.S. District Court at Las Cruces, N.M. Las Cruces is far from Albuquerque, where Federal court for New Mexico is usually held, and even farther from Echo Amphitheater. Moving the trial 366 miles south was the idea of the prosecution, which feared that in Albuquerque, let alone farther north, there were too many sympathizers of the Alianza for the government to get a "hanging" jury.

U.S. District Judge Howard C. Bratton conducted the Las Cruces trial. In the selection of the jury, Judge Bratton took over questioning of the talesmen, an unheard of procedure in that court. ("A master stroke that sliced through days of legal red tape," stated the Albuquerque *Tribune* of November 7,

1969.) As a rule, prospective jurors are examined by the opposing counsel. He had also issued an order forbidding parties to the case to engage in public discussion of it, and had cited two of the defendants, Reies Tijerina and Jerry Noll, for violating his injunction. Judge Bratton is a former chairman of the Public Lands Commission; his wife is an owner of disputed land.

The Federal government's choice for the trial, Las Cruces, is the second city of New Mexico. The chief industries are the aerospace and missile developments of the U.S. Armed Forces at nearby White Sands Missile Range and Holloman Air Force Base. Judge Bratton chose all the jurors in the first afternoon of the trial from a panel of 60 talesmen, one-third of whom were government employees. Those chosen included three women from Alamogordo, the home of the Air Force Base.

Shortly before the trial was called, the Las Cruces area was papered with free copies of a pamphlet by Alan Stang, professional alarm-ringer for the John Birch Society, entitled "Reies Tijerina: The Communist Plan to Grab the Southwest." On the eve of the trial, an editorial in a local paper referring to it stated that it was time to put a stop to "proponents of violence in our country."[1]

In this trial, Reies Tijerina first had the opportunity to describe to a court his life of struggle, culminating in his leading the fight for the alienated lands of the Mexicans in the Southwest. The seizure of the Echo Amphitheater campground, he had said at that time, was to bring the land grant cases before the public and into the courts, and now he had done both—although it was not in his plan that the court case should be on criminal charges against himself and his followers.

The trial also saw the first of several appearances by witnesses including David Cargo, the Governor of New Mexico, who would describe to judges and juries the deprived situation of the inhabitants of northern New Mexico.

Governor Cargo testified that "there is no dialogue between the people of northern New Mexico and the Forest Service." He detailed grievances of the Spanish Americans in the region, suffering, he said, from "bad roads, poor educational systems, trouble with disease and unemployment." He indicated that the presence of Forest Service personnel not indigenous to the area, and non-Spanish speaking, only aggravated the situation in the North.

Professor Clark Knowlton, then head of the sociology department of the University of Texas at El Paso, described the situation of the Spanish Americans in northern New Mexico as a "disgrace to the entire nation."

"They have taken all they can and will take no more," said Knowlton. He referred to Reies Tijerina as "one of the most important leaders of the Spanish Americans in the Southwest."

Charles Driscoll, leading the counsel for the defense, told the court, "Our evidence will be based on the history of a community of Spanish-speaking Americans whose families have lived there for many, many years. . . . They have the feeling that they have been deprived of their rights and that Forest Service officials are responsible.

"The government had known for months that they would present their claim in the hope that it would be brought into court. We will show that from 200 to 300 people were in that area, when one of the forest rangers panicked and made a run for the truck. [The truck contained a pistol.]

"In order to prevent a possible homicide, Reies Tijerina moved in to try to simmer down that crowd. Evidence will show that the trucks were never touched by any of these five defendants.

"Arrogance of the forest rangers provoked the crowd. Reies acted with great prudence that day."

Tijerina on the witness stand told how he had organized the Alianza while working as a church janitor in Albuquerque. The Alianza had not moved a court case itself, he said, because it lacked the money for such expensive proceedings. Its aim, instead, was to have the government assume the cost and burden of proof involved in initiating a lawsuit. This was the main purpose of the Echo Amphitheater occupation. "We thought they would serve us with an eviction notice, or something like that."

"Now that the claims are known all over the world, I think that a judge would have to think twice before he would refuse to consider them."

A professional process server testified that in advance of the encampment, Tijerina had hired him to serve a paper on Regional Forester William D. Hurst. The paper notified Hurst that the Pueblo San Joaquín del Río Chama would occupy National Forest land on October 15, and that "heirs of the land grants are fully resolved to exercise their land grant rights."

Attorney Driscoll accused Hurst of "despising" Spanish-speaking people, and refusing to allow Spanish to be spoken in his office. Hurst replied that he found Spanish-speaking people "delightful—what little contact we have had." (Hurst is stationed in Albuquerque, where over a third of the population is Mexican-American.)

After a week-long trial, the jury returned a verdict convicting all the defendants. The two who actually "hustled" the Rangers were out of jail in two months, but Reies was sent to the penitentiary on a charge of "aiding and abetting" an assault on a federal officer.

The El Paso *Times* said in its report: "The trial of the five in Doña Ana County courthouse drew more interest than any trial here since the Cricket Coogler murder case twenty years ago. Dozens of law enforcement officers and FBI agents lined the courtroom. Many residents from the northern part of New Mexico came to Las Cruces. Some stayed in motels, others camped out with bedrolls.

"Thus another chapter in the incredible history of Spanish colonization in North America is written."

While appeals from the assault convictions were being taken, Reies Tijerina and Jerry Noll underwent a two-day trial in U.S. Court for "contempt" of Judge Bratton. Both were charged with making speeches denouncing the Echo Amphitheater prosecution at the Alianza convention in October 1967. These speeches were illegally taped by police, who bugged the convention sound system.

Tijerina's remarks, made in Spanish, were translated, after a fashion, by a detective:

"We know that the judge has taken the power in his own hands. We know that the judge is using the law to drink our blood and humiliate our race."

Tijerina called eight witnesses to show that the convention was a private one, limited to members and invited guests from the Hopi and Táos Indian people and Black Power groups.

The government attorneys dwelt on the "dangers" of inviting Black Power visitors to Albuquerque, their justification for infiltrating detectives.

His talk, Tijerina testified, was designed to encourage witnesses to take the stand at the forthcoming trial in Las Cruces.

Actions of government agents, including Forest Rangers, FBI and state police, had "terrorized and frightened the hearts of the Spanish American," said Tijerina, to the point that few were at first willing to testify against the Forest Rangers. "That is the spirit that is developed over 120 years when people have lost all their money and their homes. Innocent people become weak, pale, their joints freeze."

Tijerina said that although "we have taught people what their rights are, many are on welfare, and fear they will be removed, and many have been removed."

Asked why he himself was not afraid to take the stand, Reies replied, "My life has been developed around struggle. But I know that their historic background can make our members intimidated. When it comes to courts, they see them only as death-traps. My dad used to tell me not to challenge the ranchers, not to speak to the man who grew the beets or cotton we had to work."

Sharp questions from the U.S. Attorney concerning the reason why Ralph Featherstone* of SNCC and other black leaders had been invited to the convention brought the following reply:

"There is no reason why peoples who are both oppressed should fight each other. I thought it wise to make a treaty with them. The white people must now face up to the consequences of bringing them here in chains." An aim of the Alianza, he said, is to secure equal rights for the people it represents. "That is the reason we have ties with other organizations that have the same objectives."

Judge Ewing Kerr found Tijerina and Noll guilty and gave them 30-day jail sentences and fines of $500. The U.S. Supreme Court in December 1969 refused to hear their appeal.

While the legal machinery on the Las Cruces convictions proceeded, Tijerina made a bold announcement. He would make a citizens' arrest of Judge Warren E. Burger when the latter came before the Senate Judiciary Committee for confirmation. Burger was considered President Nixon's choice of a "law and order" Chief Justice. At the hearing in Washington in June 1969, the only public criticism of his appointment came from Tijerina, who appeared at the open door of the hearing room, held behind a red velvet rope by armed police.

While the judge took flight, guided through a back door by Senator Eastland, Reies told an audience of about a hundred that he had found eight cases where Burger ruled against the constitutional rights of the poor and minorities. That afternoon he filed a citizen's warrant with the Supreme Court for the arrest of its future Chief Justice.

The Echo Amphitheater challenge did not "go up" as Reies had hoped. When the Supreme Court convened in October under the new Chief Justice, its first act was to deny the Alianza defendants a review. When he heard the news, Tijerina commented, "The U.S. Government is afraid to face the Treaty of Guadalupe Hidalgo."

* Ralph Featherstone was killed by a bomb while on his way to the trial of Rap Brown at Ellicott City, Maryland in 1970.

With Reies Tijerina already behind bars, the other four defendants surrendered to begin serving their sentences.

IT'S HARD TO FIGURE AN ANGLO

THE DISPARAGERS of Tijerina attempt to picture him as a charlatan on the order of the "Baron of Arizona," the notorious
swindler who enriched himself by claiming to be the heir of
"Spanish land" and a noble title.

On the contrary, Tijerina himself has been a victim of fak-
ers of this variety. As a general rule, he takes people at face
value, and welcomes support from where it is offered. Rarely
is he deceived by a Mexican. But Anglo-Americans appearing
in the guise of friends, and perhaps as experts in some line,
have gotten through his guard more than once.

His limited experience with "friendly" Anglos had not
taught Reies to deal with individuals like Jerry Noll, who first
attached himself to the Alianza headquarters claiming to be
an attorney, later permitted himself to be reduced to a "law
student," and was finally revealed as having gained his legal
knowledge while in jail for petty crimes in his home town of
Seattle.

As "King of the Indies," Noll made speeches at Alianza
meetings, wrote letters to the newspapers in an imitation of
legal phraseology, and on one occasion in the Legal Notices issued a lengthy declaration of war against the "foreign occu-
pants" of New Mexico, in which all opponents would be tried
by a military tribunal and executed.[2] All this was considered
irresistibly funny by the Alianza. Meanwhile Noll lived rent-
free at the Alianza office, carrying out a few clerical tasks,
while his laundry and mending were cared for by Alianza
women.

At the 1967 convention Noll delivered one extravagant
"King of the Indies" routine after another. "Oh, how we
laughed," Isabel García remembered. At the Echo Amphitheater encampment he served as judge at the mock trial of

the Forest Service men, enjoying himself immensely. It was fun for the King, and sometimes for the members, but in the long run damaging to Tijerina and his cause. The jester really was a con man, and his presence helped those interested in representing the whole organization in that light.

This tendency to error in judging Anglos could work the other way. Beverly Axelrod, a brilliant and courageous San Francisco lawyer (to whom Eldridge Cleaver dedicated his *Soul on Ice*) left her practice there, including the defense of Huey Newton, to come to New Mexico to head the Alianza's legal work. At Tijerina's request, she moved to Santa Fe with her two sons early in 1968. There she rented a little house, put up the poster of Huey with his feet on a tiger rug, and under the poster placed the same tall wicker chair in which he was pictured. She plunged into the defense of Tijerina with devoted energy, planning the many trials like a general working out a campaign for battle. She worked without cease, hardly eating, sleeping on the floor wherever she happened to be.

She handled with dignity the fury and abuse of judges who resented her unwavering vigilance on behalf of her clients, and appeared deaf to their shouts of "Sit down!" as she got the vital objections into the record. A people's lawyer, she aroused in the opposing counsel all their latent anti-Semitism and hatred of intelligent women. No professional across-the-table camaraderie was extended to her. Even the customary fee due her as a court-appointed attorney was reduced.

Mrs. Axelrod went to jail for contempt with an armful of books and the smiling comment that it was a good chance to catch up with her rest and reading.

In the fall of 1968 there appeared at Alianza headquarters civil rights lawyer William Higgs of Mississippi, disbarred in that state. Although unable to argue cases in court, Higgs served as legal adviser in the Alianza office with unquestionable skill. He also showed a fondness for adventurist schemes in which he did not take part, such as the burning of the For-

est Service signs at Coyote. This incident, in which Tijerina
nearly lost his life, and later was sentenced to three years in
Federal prison, was hinted at by Higgs to the Albuquerque
Journal several days before it happened, when he told the
newspaper ("giggling," the report said) that "something unusual" would happen at Coyote on the weekend.[3]

The services of Higgs cost the Alianza the courtroom assistance of Beverly Axelrod. Tijerina placed his confidence in
Higgs, and Mrs. Axelrod was elbowed out of legal decision-
making. Higgs' apparent dislike of women extended in particular to a brilliant lawyer who opposed some of his plans.
There was nothing for her to do but leave.

The struggle in New Mexico is sometimes seen as a battle
between "Chicanos" and "Anglos," but the actual situation is
more complex. Closer to reality is the Alianza concept of
"rich against poor." La Raza has its share of sellouts, known
as *"vendidos."* These may achieve positions of political prominence but do not share in the ruling financial strata.

Although Tijerina at times found Anglos a convenient target for polemics, in practice he distinguished between friend
and foe. In 1963 he had come into Professor Knowlton's office
in El Paso to ask the sociologist's permission to reprint a study
of land losses in New Mexico, and called on him thereafter as
a defense witness when the movement was under attack. Dr.
Frances Swadesh, whose detailed knowledge of land grants is
second only to Tijerina's, is valued by the Alianza as an expert witness with unimpeachable academic standing and the
courage to take the stand when necessary.

Attorney Axelrod once asked Tijerina: "Do you feel that
you and your people hate Anglos?" Reies replied: "No,
some of my advisers are Anglos. However, I believe racist individuals are evil. Every race has their number of evil people,
and my fight, my struggle makes it appear I hate Anglos.
Maybe it is the English language that is imposed in the
United States. But it is not a question of Anglos. Behind the
DA (Sanchez) are both (Attorney General) Boston Witt and
Senator Montoya."

7. Tierra Amarilla

TIERRA AMARILLA does not fit the stereotype of "dusty adobe village" often applied to it after the events of June 1967. Lying under the San Juan range, which is the rainspout of northern New Mexico, it is more likely to be muddy than dusty in the summer, and is often under heavy snow in winter. Twenty miles to the east, the San Juans rise to over 10,000 feet at the Plaza Nutria, where the highway crosses the mountain ridge to the Rio Grande valley. Within sight of Tierra Amarilla to the northeast are Brazos Peak and the spectacular sheer walls of Brazos Cañon. These shelter expensive hunting and fishing lodges, of which, naturally, the Tierra Amarilla people have not seen the inside, unless they were repairing the ceiling.

Tall stands of stately ponderosa pine and Engelmann spruce extend down the mountain slopes toward the town. Deer, bear, and elk abound in the woods, as do partridge and pheasant in the meadows. Some Tierra Amarilla inhabitants eat meat only when they have bagged one of these creatures. The Apache from the nearby Jicarilla Reservation make similar use of the game.

The village resembles no other in the United States, nor in the world, probably. The buildings are mainly of wood, with peaked roofs, which are the exception in New Mexico. About half are boarded up and deserted. Some of the houses are of enormous size, leading one to believe that he is seeing old hotels or perhaps lumbermen's boarding houses. But you will be told that all of them are, or were, private homes, and if you ask why so big, the answer is, "Because they had big families."

Around half-past seven in the morning, the daily bus arrives from Santa Fe, whence it has been churning for three hours or so. It leaves the mail and whatever passengers there are at the grocery and post office, and continues to Chama, 15 miles north.

Soon after, the daily gathering of the men for mail and visiting takes place at the post office. They wait, chatting while the mail is sorted. If it is a pleasant day, some may linger outside for an hour or so afterward. A word of English is seldom heard.

Just west of the Courthouse, the solitary paved street curves past the grade school before joining US 84, running north to Colorado. On the corner are the U&R Cafe, garage, and gas station, and the Emerald saloon, all enterprises of a single family. (The liquor license of the Emerald, however, belongs to former DA Alfonso Sanchez.) They and the Courthouse are nearly the only "businesses" left in Tierra Amarilla. If court is being held, all concerned must crowd into the cafe for their noon meal.

West of US 84 is the road to El Vado dam and reservoir, and a little way out this road is the new high school. It resembles a small, highly efficient new factory, but is named Escalante, for the priest who in 1776 passed this way with the first official party of Spanish to traverse the present Four Corners area (the meeting point of New Mexico, Arizona, Utah and Colorado).

The Grant

HARDSHIPS CAUSED by Forest Service policies were prompting the villagers of northern New Mexico to join the Alianza in increasing numbers. Their claims, dramatized at Echo Amphitheater, had received little notice, but less than a year later the "shoot-out" at Tierra Amarilla made headlines around the world.

Few were aware of the forces smoldering over the years that erupted in the explosion at Tierra Amarilla. Like at San Joaquín, they were kindled by a losing struggle to preserve the basis of village communal life against land stealers, private and Federal.

The application for the grant from Mexico, dated 1832, had been signed by petitioner Manuel Martinez on behalf of himself, his eight sons, and "others who want to accompany me," the usual form of application for a community grant. In the granting documents Mexico clearly referred to the communal character of the tenure. Mention was made of the "settlements" on the land and the fact that the tract would sustain up to 500 families (nearly 3,000 people) ; the grant made by Mexico was to "petitioners," plural, not just to Martinez.

But a government translator, David Whiting, falsified the translation of the original application to read, "and others who *may desire* to accompany me," thus making it appear to be an application for an individual grant which could be sold by its owner. Whiting's mistranslation of this key document was put before congressmen opposed in principle to communal land tenure. The distorted translation enabled them to promulgate an erroneous statement of who were, in fact, the grantees—not all the settlers who came with Martinez, but his immediate family alone.

Consequently, although the original Martinez had died, Congress in 1860 confirmed the grant to him only, ignoring the rights of all the other families. His son Francisco also died, and after Francisco's death his widow and heirs sold their interest to Thomas B. Catron for $4,000, a fraction of its value. But they were in desperate need of money after paying the cost of what Catron told them was a worthless investigation of their title. The fact that the patent for the entire grant had been approved by Washington was concealed from the family for years, and Catron secretly bought up interest in the grant from various heirs for as little as $164.

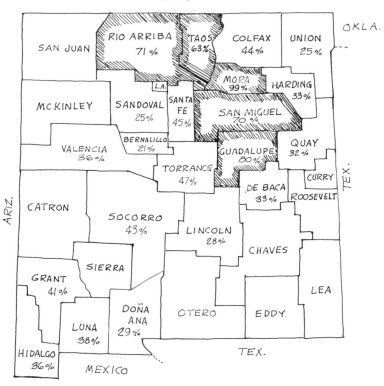

Map of New Mexico indicating percentage of Mexican Americans in each county. The five northern counties with the shaded boundaries have majority Mexican populations. The Alianza has its greatest strength in these areas, where the land-grant communities have maintained themselves most successfully.

Moreover, the receipt for the patent had been signed by Catron, although at that time he did not own any of the land. This must have involved collusion in Washington, because legally only a direct heir could receive the patent. He eventually got possession of nearly all the grant—over 500,000 out of some 586,000 acres.

Four generations have passed, and the impoverished heirs still farm what is left of the Tierra Amarilla grant. The many descendants of the Martinez family and the other grantees who have remained in the area are supporters of the Alianza, and some are defendants in the trials resulting from their struggle.

In early 1967 the New Mexico Game and Fish Department "bought" 4,000 acres of the Tierra Amarilla grant for use as an elk-feeding range—closing off the best of what grazing land remained. This shocking event brought practically the whole population—an overflow crowd of 500—to the County Courthouse on May 14, 1967. They had come to hear Tijerina, and their mood was high, militant and hopeful. There was loud assent as the Alianza leader proclaimed:

"The United States is trespassing in New Mexico, and the Tierra Amarilla grant belongs to the heirs. That is why this courtroom will not hold all the people today. You have come because you believe in your heritage. You have suffered 118 years of fear. Now it is over."

Concerning the Game and Fish purchase, he said, "According to the documents, the state's title is no good. No court has ever ruled that the Tierra Amarilla grant is not valid."

Reies spoke from the judge's bench of the courtroom that Sunday afternoon, a typically bold gesture the audience enjoyed. As was his custom, he spoke in Spanish, treating his audience to the gamut of emotions for over an hour. He jollied, wheedled, scolded, counseled, accused, explained, ridiculed and exhorted.

"I am not standing here to send some poor innocent to the

pen," said Reies, "but to emphasize that the people are the government, the people are the state. In 1832 this land was set aside for the population of a village. It is time now to reestablish government by the people of Tierra Amarilla."

Because of the "cloudy" condition of the titles, the village of Tierra Amarilla has not been incorporated to this day, although it is the county seat. It is governed by the county courthouse clique who would be chief witnesses against Tijerina in the ensuing trials.

That May afternoon Alianza members took the floor to explain that the stolen land was not their only grievance. They denounced the local schools, where the speaking of Spanish was severely suppressed. Reies assured them that the state had no authority to deny children their language. He quoted the Protocol signed at the end of the war with Mexico, where their rights were pledged.

"They extend to the language and culture of the people," he emphasized, "as well as guaranteeing the land."

"The land thieves abuse the Spanish language, abuse our culture, abuse our property. Here in New Mexico the law requiring teachers to be competent in Spanish is ignored. To correct all these abuses we must elect men who represent the people. Together we are the government. We must elect men who are brave and a little angry."

The Alianza then proceeded to choose Mexican-style officials from among the heirs to carry out the administrative duties of the town. Six officers were nominated from the floor and unanimously elected by the 67 direct heirs to the grant who were present. Hardy, tanned farmers and workers, they were formally sworn in and seated in the jury box, headed by Juan Martinez, "who has twelve sons to serve you."

A conference and public rally was announced, to be held in the Coyote schoolyard three weeks later. All were urged to be there and take part in planning the struggles ahead.

"The State Police is working hard to divide us," Tijerina said. "They are offering to pay people to start trouble. We do not want violence," he warned, "but they had better not touch us."

It had been raining, but now the mountain shower passed, and the crowd left the stuffy courtroom with relief to walk to the ball park nearby. Old people and their sons and daughters stood or squatted by the fence, while Reies delivered a summary of his earlier speech, this time in English to CBS microphones set up for a Walter Cronkite "special." Heirs to the land stepped forward to speak forcefully of the grievances and their determination to reclaim their rights. But the program never was seen, at least not in New Mexico.

The powerful began to show signs of panic when it appeared that Tijerina might actually be leading the grantees to regain what was theirs. Because of the beauty of the ten million stolen acres? No—because the value of what it produced had suddenly increased. Commercial lumber prices multiplied sixfold, and most of it was concentrated in the Coyote area on the San Joaquín grant. Timber taken from grant lands in the Santa Fe Forest in 1968 alone brought $28 million.

But far greater were the riches that lay below the land. There was an impelling urgency to increase the mining of uranium, since the Atomic Energy Commission had turned over nuclear production to private industry, and it was well known that New Mexico has the largest nuclear reserves in the country. In 1967 the AEC itself bought a million pounds of uranium concentrate from four New Mexico mills at a cost of $75 million.[1] With the expansion in nuclear power reactors, big oil companies like Standard, Gulf, and Atlantic Richfield were attracted into the uranium business. Uranium prospecting was in progress on land claimed by the grantees north of Ghost Ranch, and many mineral leases were filed by major companies in the vicinity of the Tierra Amarilla grant. "There's a lot of extravagant optimism involved," said an editorial in the *New Mexican*.

There was also a lot of political pressure involved. Millionaire Richard Bokum II, former Princeton fullback who made his fortune in New Mexico uranium, was only one of the promoters powerful in the State's Democratic Party.

COUNTER-OFFENSIVE

THE DRIVE to destroy the Alianza began that Spring, when a Federal judge ordered Tijerina to hand over its membership lists. Hoping to avoid persecution of their members, the elders disbanded the Alianza Federal de Mercedes (Federal Alliance of Land Grants) and replaced it with a new organization —the Alianza Federal de Pueblos Libres (Federal Alliance of Free Communities).

The pressure mounted, and the Coyote conference set for June 3 never took place. District Attorney Alfonso Sanchez moved early to forestall it. His warning assaulted the ears of radio listeners all week and was distributed as a leaflet by police throughout northern New Mexico: "As D.A. I wish to give notice that said meeting is against the law. Criminal charges will be filed against all those who attend. Penalty five years in the penitentiary. You are being misled by Reies Lopez Tijerina. What he professes is Communist and is illegal. Stay home and do not attend."

The village of Coyote is located within the San Joaquín land grant, and the local families had prepared for a barbecue and meeting to last all weekend. But State Police reinforcements were sent to the area Friday night, June 2. They set up a roadblock on the main highway, and when the advance party of the Alianza showed up next morning, arrests began. Cars were searched, belongings seized, including the Alianza membership files. Before the meeting was scheduled to begin, eleven men had been arrested and charged with unlawful assembly.

The bulk of the Alianza members who were headed for Coyote, warned of what was taking place there, sheered off and went instead to Canjilón, a hamlet in the foothills above

Tierra Amarilla. Being prepared for a weekend of camping, the families went to stay on the farm of Tobías Leyba, a leader of the Alianza. Indignation ran high among the campers over the breaking-up of their meeting at Coyote, their resentment particularly fixed on District Attorney Sanchez as the person mainly responsible for the denial of their right to meet. They felt that Sanchez had a personal motive for trying to smash their organization. A member was sent back to Albuquerque to get a copy of the law on citizen's arrest and some warrants.

Uvaldo Velasquez, who had been ordered by Sanchez to lock the Coyote hall, later described the DA's disruption of Alianza plans:*

"All the people knew about the meeting on June 3rd. I was in charge of the Coyote Center that used to be a public school, and I had a key to the place. People from all around were invited to the meeting. But on the second of June, I had orders from DA Sanchez that said, 'Do not open the place for the meeting.' The next day on the third I went over to the Center and there were cops all over."

Tijerina: "Did you know what the meeting was about?"

Velasquez: "An Alianza get together. We would write a letter to the President of the United States to investigate if the grants were ours."

Assistant District Attorney E. E. Chavez cross-examined: "Isn't it a fact that the main purpose of the Alianza is to try to get back Tierra Amarilla land grant and set up a separate state and take over this land?"

Velasquez: "No, sir. We were going to make a petition to the President to give us justice in our land."

The campers soon learned that the District Attorney had not confined himself to arresting people on their way to the Coyote meeting. On its eve police had conducted a night-time roundup of those heirs to the Tierra Amarilla grant who had

---

* Testimony at Tijerina's trial, Bernalillo County Courthouse, December 6, 1968.

been elected at the courthouse meeting on May 14. Old men were not allowed to look for their glasses and others hardly given time to dress. One of these was Sam Benavídez, a carpenter. He related:

"That night on the second day of June they arrested me. . . . I was taken down to Santa Fe, 110 miles." He was never informed of the charge, but thought he was arrested because he had been claiming his land. Tijerina asked him:

"Do you feel that you have been robbed of your land grants?" Benavídez answered, "Yes." And when Tijerina asked him how long he had been complaining about his rights, Benavídez replied: "Twenty or twenty-five years. Before, we had Mr. Alfonso Sanchez as lawyer. We collected money for him and so did the G.I. Forum."*

Tijerina: "Do you know why he quit?"

Benavídez: "He wanted more money, we didn't have it. He got more money from the others."†

Mrs. Gregorita Aguilar, wife of Cruz Aguilar and mother of eight children, is a small delicate-looking woman with a face like a cameo. On the day she testified, her long hair was held back by a white band. She spoke through an interpreter, and sometimes straightened him out.

"I went to Coyote," she said, "but the roads were blocked by officers. There were a few people there when I arrived. I told them I was mad because they jailed my husband. They had no warrant. They shot the ceiling in my house. They saw I was expecting a baby and didn't care about it. One of the men pushed me and I went and got a rifle from the truck."

Tijerina: "Why did you do that?"

---

* Mexican American organization founded by Dr. Hector Garcia of Texas.
† Sanchez affirmed that he had represented 100 heirs to the Tierra Amarilla Grant in 1958 in a suit against the Payne Land & Livestock Co., but dropped it before it came to trial. The Company won the case. These circumstances were revealed in the Albuquerque *Journal* of August 8, 1967.

Mrs. Aguilar: "Because I would arrest even the President if he didn't present an order when he came on my land."

Mrs. Aguilar then told of how police "came June 5th to ask me for minutes of the meeting in the courthouse," so as to arrest those who were elected officers at that time. She related that she had known the Alianza about six years. "Before that my husband and father-in-law were fighting for their land. They got the land away from my husband's father."

In the dragnet, police picked up many members of the Alianza on trumped up charges of "killing a deer," and were reportedly looking for Reies with such a warrant. But as happens in a dragnet, it yielded an unexpected catch.

This was Alfonso Chavez, a short man with pronounced eyebrows. He lives in Albuquerque and is a mechanic and welder. He had been working for a highway contractor at Tierra Amarilla. He is not a member of the Alianza. Said Chavez: "On the third of June the DA sent for me and charged me with 27 different counts. One of them was extortion against the government. Twenty policemen with shotguns arrested me on the job. They told me then it was for 'killing animals.' "

Tijerina: "Have you ever been tried on those counts?"

Chavez: "No, they locked me up four or five different times, but I was never prosecuted. The criminal complaint was signed by DA Alfonso Sanchez 'With intent to wrongfully obtain land from the government, unlawfully assembled to take over lands from the U.S.'

"They said in Santa Fe that I was the main leader, the main Communist. Scared my wife to death, my wife is blind. I was fired and I have been out of a job ever since. Tijerina man, here's your check, out you go.

"In Tierra Amarilla one night a policeman asked me about Alianza and meetings. He asked me about Tijerina. I said he's got more brains in his toes than you got in your head. Maybe that is the reason I was arrested."

8. The Courthouse Raid

TIJERINA DESCRIBED the intensive week that preceded the courthouse fracas as follows:*

"The papers were using the declarations of the 'King of the Indies' (Noll) to create fear among Anglos, although we have never officially supported his claim. They were spreading the rumor that this so-called King and 'Tiger' Tijerina were taking over the Southwest."

Tipped off by a reporter that DA Sanchez had met secretly with state police and decided to arrest him and other Alianza leaders on false charges, Reies went to the North.

"I changed from place to place. Sometimes cars in twos and threes arrived at a house asking where I was. I was convinced Mr. Al Sanchez was the victim of his own enthusiasm. His name was before the press and he was stating that we had no legal grounds to either the San Joaquín or Tierra Amarilla land grants."

Widespread reports reached Tijerina that Sanchez and the state police were trying to find an excuse to kill him.

"I was surrounded by a fabrication, a psychological ambush. I called the Albuquerque *Tribune* and the *Journal,* asking them to publish an article by Herrera, 'Tijerina the Moses of the Mexican-American,' that appeared in the Denver and El Paso papers. It answered the wild stories they were printing. They said, 'We print what we want.' I was up against a psychological, legal, economic wall that I had no strength to overcome.

"When my wife came to where I was, I scolded her. She said

* Testimony at Bernalillo County Courthouse, December 10, 1968.

she could not stand to stay in Albuquerque. 'I can't sleep. Phone calls continuously, Where is Tijerina? The windows surrounded by detectives every night.'

"I heard information Mr. Sanchez would not rest until he got the big fish. I told my wife to go to Canjilón. The Forest Rangers were helping Mr. Sanchez as spies with field glasses, reporting everything that was going on.

"That morning, June 5, very early, I went to Tierra Amarilla. We had received the laws about the citizens' arrest, how legal, constitutional, powerful is this right.* I knew that the people had been taught in the last three or four years. They had learned the rights denied to them for 120 years. They had turned from ignorant people who could be kicked around by any cop into men and women who would no longer be pushed around."

On Monday, as had been announced in the newspapers, the eleven arrested at Coyote were taken to Tierra Amarilla to be arraigned before District Judge James Scarborough. It was assumed that DA Alfonso Sanchez would be present, and a group of the Alianza members who were still camping at the Leyba farm decided to go to the courthouse and make a citizens' arrest of the District Attorney for violation of their civil rights at Coyote.

When they arrived at Tierra Amarilla, the arraignment had just been concluded, and the eleven defendants released on bail. District Attorney Sanchez was not present, having sent an assistant.

Twenty men armed with their hunting rifles and a warrant arrived at the courthouse at about three o'clock. As they entered, four were stopped by State Patrolman Nick Saíz, who did not know them and drew his gun. Geronimo Borunda swears it was he who shot Saíz in self-defense, but the state insists that it was a member of a well-known land grant family, Juan Valdez.

The searchers ordered the courthouse employees into the

* Law on Citizens' Arrest, see Appendix.

County Commissioners' office, "so you don't get hurt," and when it became apparent that Sanchez was not in the courthouse, they left. Two men stayed behind, and when they drove off an hour later, took with them a reporter and a deputy sheriff.

In the meantime, they had called an ambulance for Saíz and sent undersheriff Dan Rivera, who had a slight head wound, to the doctor. The third wounded man, jailer Eulogio Salazar, had been jumping out a window when shot by someone in the crowd outside the courthouse, and was taken to the hospital by his family. No Alianza members were hurt.

While the arresting party went into the courthouse, Reies Tijerina waited nearby at the home of Mrs. Fernanda Martinez. Describing that day, Mrs. Martinez first spoke of her family's long efforts to regain the land.*

"In 1919 a lawyer went to the Tierra Amarilla land grant people and said he could get land freed for the people for one thousand dollars. It was Octaviano Larrazolo.† We never heard what he did."

District Attorney Alfonso Sanchez was another lawyer who had taken their money without results, she testified.

"Did you see me on June 5 in Tierra Amarilla?" asked Tijerina.

"Yes, I saw you in my house about seven in the morning. You stayed there all day and in the afternoon a little boy came in and said there was shooting at the courthouse."

On cross-examination, Mrs. Martinez was asked why she "harbored" Tijerina.

"I don't know anything about harboring," she replied, "but the police were running after him like mad wolves. They went to my house and offered to pay me a big ransom if I would tell them where Reies Lopez Tijerina was. They just wanted to put him behind bars, so they would have all the

---

* Testimony at Bernalillo County Courthouse, December 1968.
† Father of the presiding judge in the above case.

land grants for themselves . . . the state police and the Federal Government."

To return to Tijerina's account of that afternoon: "When did I go to the courthouse? The son of Cruz Aguilar had gone to the arraignment that day. He came running to the house where I was. He says, 'Mr. Tijerina, the police are shooting the people.' I had been keeping up with the news that the courthouse was surrounded by police and trouble expected, additional police cars summoned. It was easy for me to believe the State Police had charged.

"I was under torturing, cold pain. We got there, I don't know how. It took a long time to travel those two blocks to the courthouse. Some of the people outside the courthouse showed panic, fright; others showed excitement. People were saying it was an ambush.

"'Don't go in!' Not only Rose [Reies' eldest daughter], but other people told me. Members from as far as Las Vegas, Anton Chico, Santa Rosa, got in my way. Faces that stayed with me for months after that.

"When I entered the courthouse, I expected to see dead people all over. One person was standing holding a rifle in the ribs of somebody. I grabbed the rifle so hard he said, "What have I done?' Before I left I grabbed the arm of somebody. 'Get some ambulances!' I said. 'Now you have give them the excuse to kill us all—*que nos maten, que nos acaben a todos*.'* When I made sure there were no dead people or bleeding people in the offices, I left the place.

"Later in the mountains I reviewed whatever had been attached to my mind," Tijerina said.

For although he was only in the courthouse a short time, Tijerina arrived at a clear picture of what happened that afternoon. The state, in six trials, on the other hand, produced only a confused and jumbled story, becoming more contradic-

---

* "To kill us, to finish us all off." A clerk had testified that she heard Tijerina say, "*Acaben con todos*" (Finish them all off).

tory as time and prosecutions went on. The state's witnesses were, for the most part, courthouse employees, and the Río Arriba County Courthouse bestows upon the people of Tierra Amarilla the largest payroll in town. Its 30 employees, from tax assessor to typist, may each provide the only cash income for a three-generation family, and a job that must be saved at all costs.

At that time, the county Democratic machine had total control of the courthouse. Its head man was Emilio Naranjo, chairman of the County Committee, and sheriff for many years. When the Johnson administration made him a U.S. Marshal, his son Benny inherited the sheriff's badge.

But Benny did not fight the land grantees with the same ardor as his father. He threw himself on the floor that famous afternoon, concealing his badge, and as soon as it was over, blurted out to newsmen and the tv camera:

"It wasn't any jailbreak like you guys said, that's all wrong. They came here for Al Sanchez. I kept hearing them say, 'Reies said not to hurt nobody, Reies said not to hurt nobody.'

"The one who got shot [Saíz], that was because he went for his gun. . . . The raiders had it in for Alfonso Sanchez."[1]

But a policeman and a jailer were wounded, and a sheriff's deputy and a reporter allegedly "kidnapped." For the latter offense the State demanded the death penalty. In order to jail as many Alianzistas as possible, state witnesses contradicted one another, others gave testimony that conflicted with their own previous evidence. The courthouse employees began to sound like members of a repertory theater group—the same people appeared at various trials looking the same, but speaking new lines, written to fit the requirements of a script concocted to convict the current defendant.

One of the two "kidnap" victims was UPI reporter Larry Calloway. He had been called to testify for the State in the preliminary hearing, but once Tijerina was singled out as a man to be executed, the newsman's story no longer fit into their script. So that when Tijerina was tried for kidnapping, he subpoenaed Calloway as a witness for the defense.

Calloway's evidence chiefly concerned the two men who had stayed behind when the arresting party left the courthouse: Baltazar Martinez, 21, and Baltazar Apodaca, 72. Martinez, a descendant of the original owners of the Tierra Amarilla grant, was proclaimed by police to be "the most dangerous man in New Mexico." He is a self-taught artist and an admirer of Che Guevara, who likes to wear a red beret. But on a Sunday morning, Martinez can be seen walking across the fields of his little farm carrying a package of cake mix for his mother in one hand and a prayerbook in the other. During the season, Baltazar works in Arizona as a lettuce cutter.

Elderly Mr. Apodaca looks at life through deep-set, penetrating eyes in a fine, calm face. Although he farms on the outskirts of Albuquerque, he could have stepped out of the Old Testament. His scorn for Anglos and Anglo ways is not concealed, nor is his contempt for their lackeys among the State's petty officeholders. His family, seeking to protect the old man from criminal prosecution as a result of the Tierra Amarilla events, had him committed to the State Hospital in 1968. Two years later he was released as "mentally well."

Calloway is a man about thirty, and when examined by Tijerina maintained a sullen expression. He was not a willing witness for the defense, but neither was he vindictive.

He had been at Coyote June 3 and noted the mounting frustration of the people, and on Monday morning went to the courthouse in Tierra Amarilla to cover the bond hearing for those arrested that weekend. At about three he was preparing to phone a story from a booth in the courthouse hallway, when he heard the shot that felled Saíz. There was a group of people standing beside the patrolman, but he couldn't say which one had a gun.

"I dropped to the floor of the phone booth because I assumed I was in the line of fire. Following that, I heard shots outside, and people running.

"About twenty minutes after the shooting began, I saw Reies Tijerina. I had met him October 22, 1966 at the Echo Amphitheater demonstration. He was wearing a dark jacket and had a pistol in his right hand.

"He was talking, but my knowledge of Spanish is not very good. I saw him just for a few seconds."

Tijerina: "Was I aiming?"

Calloway: "No, just holding the pistol with a bent elbow. You were not shooting. I dropped to the floor again and stayed there for twenty or thirty minutes."

Next, Baltazar Martinez pushed him into the Commissioners' room.

Tijerina: "Did you see me there, Mr. Calloway?"

Calloway: "No, I didn't. The state policeman was on his back in the hall. There was blood on the floor. I was frisked at the door of the County Commissioners' office by Baltazar Martinez. I took a seat on a table at the far end of the room. About twenty people were sitting there. The men had their hands either in the air or clasped behind their backs.

"The shooting was over by that time. I looked out the window and saw an ambulance pull up in front of the courthouse. Four men who went out to help load Nick Saíz in the ambulance, came back and sat down again.

"Martinez frisked a bulky man I later found out was Deputy Sheriff Pete Jaramillo. Then both of us were taken outside the door, and our hands tied behind our backs. Martinez told us to go outside. He said to me, 'no retaliation if you want to live.' He then shot at a red bubble on top of a police car."

Calloway described how he and Jaramillo were put in a pickup truck, which was driven back and forth in the town. Shotguns and rifles were gathered up from unattended police cars and loaded into the pickup, with the assistance of passersby. The weapons were transferred to the trunk of Deputy Jaramillo's GTO, parked in front of the courthouse.

"I was told to sit in the back seat of the GTO on the left

Sketch of Deputy Sheriff
Pete Jaramillo done by
Baltazar Martinez while
Jaramillo testified in
court that Martinez had
kidnapped him.

Tessa

Burning of Forest Service sign at Coyote, N.M., June 1969.

hand side. We drove north through Tierra Amarilla into a driveway. Baltazar Martinez honked the horn. A woman came onto the porch. 'Look what I caught,' he said. " 'Trespassers,' she replied, laughing." They stopped for gas at a small station a few hundred yards from the house. "Martinez asked me if I had any money. There was a $20 bill in my billfold. The attendant brought back the change, Martinez told him to put it into the billfold and put it back in my pocket."

"We passed along the street that goes straight out of town. Martinez slowed the car and looked at a new Forest Service sign that was being built by the side of the road. We drove through Canjilón on the dirt road that leads toward the mountain. It was very muddy. A state police car came past us with four men inside. I saw it stop, and the policemen got out with rifles and took positions behind the car. Two police cars pulled into the road, blocking it. Martinez gunned the car and it became stuck in the mud.

"Then Baltazar Apodaca stepped outside the car, and told me to get out. He was holding a carbine. We backed into a muddy field in front of a church. The old man slipped in the mud. I knew I could pull my hand out of the bindings. I pulled loose and pulled the carbine away from Apodaca, and he was handcuffed by State police officers. Baltazar Martinez and Pete Jaramillo could be seen on foot in the distance."

Tijerina: "Are you sure you didn't see me carrying on a conversation with you while holding a rifle in the ribs of Jaramillo?"

Calloway: "I am certain I did not carry on a conversation with Reies Tijerina while he was holding a rifle in the ribs of Pete Jaramillo."

Tijerina: "You were called by the state to testify in Santa Fe? ["Yes."] Do you know why you were left out this time? ["No"].*

* From Calloway's testimony at preliminary hearing February 5, 1968 and at Bernalillo County Courthouse trial in December 1968.

At the preliminary hearing, Deputy Sheriff Jaramillo's evidence was essentially the same as Calloway's, until the point when they reached Canjilón. Speaking through an interpreter, Jaramillo said:

"It was about five o'clock when we got to Canjilón, twenty miles from Tierra Amarilla. Baltazar Martinez had me in front of him and was using me as a shield with the State Police. He backed me all the way across the churchyard and right in front of the post office. There was a green Dodge with three kids sitting in the front seat. He ordered this kid to drive toward the mountains."

At this point Baltazar Martinez' mother appeared and began remonstrating with her son. Police yelled at her to get out of the way, but instead she got into the car.

"There were three kids, Baltazar's mother and Baltazar. We drove toward the mountains about five miles out of Canjilón. Then he let me out of the car. His mother told him to turn me loose and give himself up."

Instead, Martinez ran the puffing Jaramillo across a field, quickly left him behind, and took off into the mountains.

The other members of the citizens' arrest party had disappeared long since, pursued by Forest Rangers acting as bloodhounds for the State Police.

THE SHEEP PEN

PICNICKERS AT the Leyba farm at Canjilón, on the evening of the courthouse fracas, were descended upon by an armed force of hundreds. The size of the brigade revealed the panic into which the authorities had been thrown.

State police, the New Mexico Mounted Patrol, Forest Service rangers, policemen from the Jicarilla Apache Reservation, and a battalion of the National Guard all converged on Canjilón. They surrounded the wooded pasture of the Leybas, where about 60 women, children and older men were camping on private property.

The National Guard brought a number of 40mm. gun carriages, referred to as "tanks" in the newspaper stories, and shown in news photos all over the world. Mrs. Tobias Leyba, frightened to see one of these sinister-looking vehicles crunch into her front yard, fled through the back door carrying her baby, the older children hurrying the toddlers through the brush and up the mountain side.

The campers were marched out of the grove like prisoners of war, and confined for 26 hours in a muddy sheep pen near the Leyba house. It rained that night, and their barbecue, left unattended, had burned, so there was nothing to eat, and they were without clean water. Guards followed Rose Tijerina and other young women to the outdoor toilet that had no door.

When Patsy, Tijerina's young wife, asked a National Guard officer why they were being held, he said that it was in the hope of luring back their men. She sought permission to shelter her baby from the rain, but was refused.

A writer from Albuquerque, Bill Olson, drove to Canjilón that day, encountering three police road blocks "as well as the muzzles of some ugly-looking automatic weapons."

"Convoys hurried officiously through the valley," he wrote. "Two helicopters and an airplane circled with eagle eyes." He met a convoy of police, guardsmen and mounted patrolmen. "The 'mounties' wore Stetsons and Douglas MacArthur sunglasses and carried automatic rifles. The group stopped at the now-infamous prisoner compound, arrested Rose Tijerina, and moved on to Tierra Amarilla with her to file charges."[2]

Rose, who was 18, and seven others were held without bail. Sanchez said he would not release Rose until her father surrendered.

Next afternoon most of those detained were released, but others, including Patsy Tijerina, were taken down to jail in Santa Fe. Seven-month old Isabel Tijerina was placed in care of county welfare authorities, while her mother remained in jail, and Rose in the state penitentiary.

A week later, frantic parents enlisted the help of the ACLU in a search for six teen-age boys and girls who had been held in juvenile detention for nine days, incommunicado. Thirteen of the adults held prisoner later sued District Attorney Sanchez, State Police Chief Black, and General Jolly of the National Guard, but obtained no damages from these officials.

That week a Santa Fe newsman, Peter Nabokov, was driven, blindfolded, up to Tijerina's mountain hideout so the land-grant leader could give his side of the story to the press. Tijerina, wearing a clean pressed shirt and speaking calmly, told Nabokov:

"One thing the public doesn't know is that a well organized plan by the state police has been in operation for several months, to assassinate me." The plan, he said, was spurred by the "bankers who would destroy me, my name and reputation. They are not afraid of my guns or money, because they know I don't have any."

About the raid, Tijerina said: "The Coyote meeting was planned as an orderly convention of people from all over. Not only New Mexico, but Colorado, Texas, and California. The people became furious when it was stopped, and when they learned that Alfonso Sanchez was arresting those who had attended the meeting May 14 in Tierra Amarilla. Knowing that my life was in danger, and that Alfonso Sanchez was proceeding in such an uncivilized manner, I became very strongly suspicious that they wanted to get rid of me for good. In a short meeting attended by about 75 people, we decided we had to make a citizens' arrest of the person who was tampering and abusing our constitutional rights, Mr. Al Sanchez.

"The arresting party went throughout the various rooms of the courthouse, but Al Sanchez could not be found."[3]

After Nabokov's story was published, DA Sanchez came to the newspaper office, fished the reporter's notes out of a garbage can in the alley, and threatened to arrest him and his editor, Walter Kerr, for refusing to reveal the source of their information.

Sanchez then released a map he said was confiscated from the car of Cristóbal Tijerina on June 2, to support his claim that the north was about to be taken over by "Castro-type Tijerina terrorists."

In the North, the police brought in hunting dogs as well as helicopters, but although a ferocious search ensued, not one of the "fugitives" was found. One by one, they all returned voluntarily, taking precautions not to be killed while surrendering. Moises Morales drove to the State Police office in Española, accompanied by his wife and father-in-law. While the FBI sought him in an extensive manhunt, Cristóbal Tijerina, with his lawyer and a bondsman, walked into Judge Angel's courtroom in Santa Rosa.

Governor Cargo posted a $500 reward for Baltazar Martinez, who was reported by police to be wearing a girdle of dynamite. But when, after two months at large, Martinez turned himself in to his mother, she arranged his surrender and collected the reward. When Cargo received the canceled check, he learned that it had been signed over to Baltazar and that the "armed raider" had returned to the Tierra Amarilla courthouse—to obtain a marriage license. The wedding was one of the gayest ever recalled in Río Arriba County.

Reies Tijerina, together with his son Hugh (David) and anti-poverty worker Velasquez, were arrested by State Police in a car about ten miles from Albuquerque. Tijerina was heading home because he had become suddenly ill. Although he was in severe pain, he and his son were taken to the penitentiary after an angry confrontation with Judge Scarborough, who had been hiding in a broom closet during the Tierra Amarilla events.

While headlines read "Police Continue Mountain Search for Raid Party," a group of prominent Chicanos from Colorado demonstrated in Santa Fe. Attorney Levi Martinez, Sociology Professor Dr. Daniel Valdez, Corky Gonzales, and about 30 others took part. Attorney Martinez talked to Tijerina in the penitentiary and said, "He's in good spirits. He's sure of himself."[4] Two days later a large crowd waited for his arrival for a bail hearing at the Santa Fe Courthouse. They shouted, "Viva Tijerina!" as he alighted. Forced by the pressure of hundreds, the hearing was shifted from the judge's chambers to the courtroom, where watched by heavily armed police, Indo-Hispano men and women from all over the State offered all they owned to assure his bond. But Sanchez asserted that first degree kidnapping was not a bondable offense. "The response to the petition for bail is all full of nightmares about hand grenades, bombs, revolution by the Alianza, and no calm logical argument," said a defense attorney.

On June 15 Sanchez announced that he would ask for the death penalty against Tijerina and the other defendants. This only brought them more support. Letter columns of the newspapers were filled with expressions from local people, such as:

"Reies Lopez Tijerina will go down in history as legend in the Southwest, comparable to Pancho Villa. . . . When the law protects a large corporation in California [Wrigley's] that uses the Treaty of Guadalupe Hidalgo to escape paying taxes on Catalina Island, why is the Treaty good for a corporation and not for a large mass of people?"[5]

"The actions of Reies Lopez Tijerina opened the eyes of all of us with a desperate cry for help," said another letter.

Anglo liberals pointed out the neglect and misery prevailing in the north as the obvious cause of the blowout. Many Chicanos wrote letters similar to one by a Táos man about "the day when the native people were told they could no longer graze their cattle . . . the reason was that a company had bought the land from someone, and now was bringing in cattle from out of state . . . . This same company, the Pot Creek Lumber Co., went into the lumber business in a big way and cut millions of dollars worth of lumber out of this land . . . and people wonder how come so many of these people are on welfare."[6]

A community leader from Española wrote concerning the "ambitious District Attorney who prosecutes for personal gain, to secure a prize political office." He predicted that Sanchez' actions "had an adverse effect in the same way that public hangings in the old days produced fear and contempt rather than respect for law."[7]

Long pent-up resentments exploded in print:

"The conquerors write the history books for the purpose of instilling in minds of the young a one-sided view, suppressing facts which do not meet what the conqueror considers the invincibility of his way of life, memorializing the violent as long as it is the English-speaking who create the violence, creating the fiction that because they are white and English-speaking they are superior to the rest of mankind."[8]

A newly formed War on Poverty group asked for five million dollars for the three northern New Mexico counties, and Congressman Joseph Y. Resnick (D-NY) called a special hearing of a House Agriculture Subcommittee. Governor Cargo flew to Washington to testify that loss of grazing land—the thing they hold most dearly —to National Forest Rangers caused the people to revolt. "We begged the Forest Service again and again to let the local farmers use the grazing area, but to no avail. They prefer to let outsiders come in."

Knowlton, who had been flown to New Mexico from Texas to help abate the trouble, went on to Washington to describe the onslaughts of forest rangers. As an example, he told the committee that, to comply with Forest Service requirements for wilderness areas, sheepherders were forced to tear down their shacks and live in tents.

A congressman called the area the Watts of rural America.

Father Garcia, director of the OEO in New Mexico, saw the "raid" as a symbolic act. "The surge of people in poverty to join the Alianza stems from an innate desire to attain first-class citizenship."[9]

Congressman Resnick's subcommittee, however, was no match for the powerful U.S. Forest Service. That branch of the Department of Agriculture reacted to problems in northern New Mexico by increasing the number of rangers equipped with automatic weapons.

There were many calls for a congressional investigation of the land grants, and Sheriff Naranjo suggested formation of a commission to review the claims of Tijerina's followers so they could have "every opportunity to put up or shut up." Tijerina answered from the penitentiary that Naranjo's put up or shut up offer "is a very good challenge. We would like to take their challenge . . . we would like to put the documents and facts on the table. We want to come before a commission where we come in and establish in a satisfactory manner our claims."[10]

The *New York Times* sent a reporter to the area, and published a highly colorful story about "insurrectionists," who held a village and "freed ten of their friends." Although his account of current events was fictitious, the *Times* man did try to interpret New Mexico in Eastern terms: "The Carson National Forest is as large as Vermont . . . . Río Arriba is Appalachia with a language problem . . . Seventy percent of its population is Spanish American and ten percent Indian. It is Spanish Harlem with clean air, cool summer nights and a population density of 4-5 persons a square mile. . . . Only a handful of ranchers with mammoth holdings seem to be able to make a living off the land."

The *Times* reporter talked to Bill Mundy of Tierra Amarilla, "a 50-year old rancher who has been in the valley sixteen years, owns 25,000 acres and is an outspoken opponent of the land granters." Mundy knew at the time he acquired the land that the land titles were not clear, but said, "I knew it was the only way I would ever get the kind of spread I wanted, so I decided to take it, freak deal, fight and all." In 1959 he won a suit filed by several heirs. Shortly after, his house burned.[11]

On June 19, Tijerina was taken to Albuquerque for a hearing on the Echo Amphitheater incident. Unprecedented security measures prevailed at the 13-story Federal Courthouse as Reies and three co-defendants drove up in cars filled with armed guards. Attired in khaki prison clothes, handcuffed and fettered together by chains around their waists, Alfonso Chavez, Ezequiel Dominguez, Jerry Noll, and Tijerina warmly greeted relatives and friends in the audience.

On the 22nd the land-grant leader left the penitentiary once more, this time for arraignment at Santa Fe. State police held short-barrelled shotguns against their thighs while he alighted, and the crowd inside pressed against the police guarding the courtroom doors. Cries of "Viva Tijerina!" were again heard from those unable to get into the courtroom. The room, with its carved *vigas,** was filled to capacity, and buzzed with Spanish as men and women in work clothes compared their experiences of the past two weeks. The prisoners, 16 men and one girl, entered single file, and Reies talked quietly to his daughter Rose and other fellow prisoners until Judge Angel opened the arraignment, saying, "The eyes of the world are on this courtroom today."

All 17 were charged with first-degree kidnapping (a capital crime), assault on a jail and assault with intent to commit murder. All pleaded not guilty.

District Attorney Sanchez became increasingly irritated as 13 were released on bail. "I can place all 17 defendants at the scene," he protested. "You haven't presented that evidence to this court today," replied the judge.

Returned to the penitentiary without bail were Reies Tijerina, Tobias Leyba, Juan Valdez, and Baltazar Apodaca. At that time, Baltazar Martinez and Cristobal Tijerina were still at large.

* Exposed roof beams.

The June 5 explosion produced far-reaching effects on the position of the Alianza. The first was increased recognition by other Mexican American groups. " 'Tierra Amarilla' had become a rallying cry as well as a place," wrote Dr. Swadesh.[12] From Denver came Rodolfo "Corky" Gonzales to hail the Alianza members. A few weeks later, Bert Corona, leader of the Los Angeles Mexican American Political Association (MAPA) made a similar pilgrimage to Albuquerque.

"César Chavez, leader of the migrant farm workers of the Southwest, was invited to Albuquerque to address liberal organizations, but took time out to attend a regular meeting of the Alianza. There, after an effusive greeting by the membership and a public embrace with Tijerina, Chavez announced that, if he were a New Mexico resident, he would join the Alianza, 'because the issue of the land is crucial to rural Mejicanos and reflects the cruel injustices to which they have been subjected.' "

Militant Anglo youth from California and the East also came to Tijerina when they heard that he had launched rebellion at Tierra Amarilla. They arrived with their bedrolls, rifles and visions of the Sierra Maestra. They were disappointed to hear that what had happened at Tierra Amarilla was a miscarriage of a citizens' arrest, and that guerrilla warfare in Río Arriba was not on the program.

The question of land grants had passed into a wider struggle, involving not only the heirs of land grants but the inheritors of oppression of a whole race. Tijerina's office was turned into a clearinghouse of pain. He had become a national figure, to march onto a larger stage than the one he occupied at Alianza headquarters.

From all over the Southwest, people sought the man with a burning conscience and a voice that the conscience made a shout.

The raid itself became the subject of many folk ballads. Even as the preliminary hearing was taking place, where the

Alianzistas were accused of 29 charges of kidnapping and intent to kill, "there were plenty of buyers for records reciting lyrical versions of the episode."[13] One of these, sold out at local Woolworth stores, was called *Corrido de Río Arriba* recorded by Los Reyes de Albuquerque.

A group of our race,
Very discontented, descended
And upon state officials
They took their revenge.

More than a dozen ballads with similar themes were written, two by prominent Alianza members.

9. Politics—New and Old

SHORTLY AFTER his release from jail, Reies went to Chicago for the New Politics Convention in September 1967. Up until then, he had avoided what he considered useless political embroilments, and was reluctant at first to make the trip. He changed his mind, however, when told that there would be an opportunity to meet and establish ties with Black leaders. As it turned out, he was merely introduced at the rally that preceded the Convention, and did not have a chance to speak on his struggle as he had been promised. But he talked with Dr. Martin Luther King at the airport, and invited him to the forthcoming Alianza Convention.

Tijerina played a dominant role on the Spanish-speaking panel, pulling together the 50 Puerto Rican and Mexican American delegates from various parts of the country, most of whom had never met.

The delegates were critical of preparations for the convention that had excluded Spanish-speaking people from planning committees, and particularly from the resolutions committee. When the chairman of this committee was confronted by a group of Mexican delegates, dissatisfied with the weak and vague resolution that dealt with their problems, and demanding the right to be heard in committee hearings, that gentleman responded apologetically, "I didn't know there were six million of them."*

The panel supported the demands of the Black Caucus, and urged that Spanish-speaking and Afro-American people be fully represented on all bodies of the New Politics movement. There was total agreement when Tijerina said:

"The situation of the Mexicans and Puerto Ricans is similar to that of the Negro people, but it is not the same. We have to fight for the right to speak our language. Even the demand of the Puerto Rican for independence is different from the Mexican's demands. But we must unite all these with the Negro, the Indian, and the 'good Anglos,' in order to change our condition."

The consensus of the panel was that "You can't play the traditional game of politics within the Democratic Party. It isn't going to change anything for people who are getting constantly poorer. But when a new party is formed, we must see to it that it includes us all."

Like it or not, Tijerina was being thrust into the political arena.

Increasing support for the Alianza angered Senator Montoya, highest ranking Mexican American in Washington. The senator, who was regarded as Lyndon Johnson's spokesman in Latin America, saw the militant organization as a threat to a political career built on collaboration.

"The last thing the Spanish-speaking need is agitation, rabble-rousing or creation of false hopes," he declared shortly

---

* Twelve million is closer to the actual figure.

after Tierra Amarilla.[1] He called Reies Lopez Tijerina an "outsider," who "sparked violence and set back racial relations,"[2] and "an enemy of the United States and a damned liar," because he had told the people of Spain that the children of the Spanish in New Mexico were hungry and lacked educational opportunities.[3]

Montoya decried the Alianza's opposition to the war. "I would certainly back any decision that might be made by the President involving more escalation of the war. I certainly favor bombing of North Vietnam," he told the *New Mexican*[4] at a time when hugely disproportionate figures of Mexican Americans killed were being published, and Tijerina was making declarations for peace from the penitentiary.

In October, Tijerina and the Senator came face to face at a meeting of MAPA in San Diego. The Senator attempted to defend both the domestic and foreign policies of the Johnson administration, but Tijerina manifested no such blind allegiance, lashing out with equal bitterness at war-makers, bankers, and the big growers as oppressors of the Spanish-speaking millions.[5]

The Senator excoriated the rapidly growing ties between the Alianza and other freedom movements. "Spanish Americans," he declared, "will make no alliances with black nationalists who hate America. We do not lie down in the gutter with Ron Karenga, Stokely Carmichael, and Rap Brown— who seek to put another wound in America's body."[6]

Senator Montoya was not unbiased in his opposition to Tijerina's land claims, having exacted land as legal fees from poor farmers more than once as a young lawyer. "Who has investigated the wondrous rags to riches climb of Joseph Montoya?" asked Jose Madríl, World War II winner of Presidential citations for bravery, and a veteran of the skirmish at Tierra Amarilla.

Montoya often represented the President at Alliance for Progress and other meetings in Latin America. His attacks on Tijerina, therefore, became particularly intemperate, calling him "a discredited charlatan, monster, racist and creature of darkness," when the land-grant leader announced plans to take the plight of New Mexicans to the United Nations, and revealed that a Washington lawyer, David Rein, was preparing documentation for that purpose. The Santa Fe *News* of January 4, 1968 published a cartoon of two cowboys discussing the news: "Looks like Sen. Montoya found out about the Alianza trouble," says one. "And it sounds like he's running against Reies Tijerina," replied the other.

DEATH OF A JAILER

ON THE morning of January 3, 1968, the battered body of Eulogio Salazar was found stuffed into his car near Tierra Amarilla. Salazar, a Río Arriba County jailer, had testified that Tijerina wounded him in the courthouse fray.

Asked if he believed the Alianza responsible for Salazar's murder, District Attorney Alfonso Sanchez said, "Of course! Who else?" and immediately drove to Las Vegas to persuade Judge Angel to revoke bonds the 20 defendants had posted in the June 5 case.*

When told of the murder, Reies Tijerina declared on TV that the people of the Alianza believe in mass popular struggle and not in bloody crimes. "This is a well financed and well organized move by some people who are against my cause." At the same time, Tijerina told the Albuquerque *Journal*, "It is very strange that this happened shortly after Senator Joseph Montoya had leveled another blast at me, because we intend to take our case to the United Nations."

Eighteen defendants in the earlier case were rounded up, mostly in Albuquerque, 160 miles from the scene of the crime. Two missed the dragnet: Baltazar Martínez working

* References in this section are from The Santa Fe *New Mexican*, January 3–14, 1968.

in Arizona, and 15-year-old Danny Tijerina, at school in Denver.

Cristóbal Tijerina was arrested in Tierra Amarilla together with Felix Martínez. Police had expected them to be in Tierra Amarilla on the night of the murder, thus placing them at the scene of the crime, as they had an appointment with the police to pick up possessions seized at Coyote. But they had driven up from Santa Fe the morning of the 3rd, instead, and when charged with murder, declared someone was out to get Reies.

The panic caused by police reprisals after the June events had subsided and most of its victims were again working. But now, just ten days before the date set for a preliminary hearing, every available medium was used to renew hysteria. State Police Chief Joe Black bellowed: "Your prime target is Reies Tijerina. Salazar was the key witness against him."

Salazar had said at a bond hearing that Tijerina shot him, but no other witness testified that Tijerina had shot anyone. The defense was allowed only a limited cross-examination at that time, as Salazar was recovering from a wound, but defense lawyers expected to prove that the jailer was lying the first time he repeated his accusation.

Cristóbal and Felix were booked for murder, but two newsmen threw a wrench into these proceedings. They swore that they had seen Cris and Felix a hundred miles away at a Santa Fe rally for Eugene McCarthy, both before and after 8:15 pm, the time fixed for Salazar's death. Felix, a non-defendant, was released but Cris, his bond revoked, joined his brother in jail.

This brought the number of Tijerinas in the penitentiary to five: Rose, her father, her uncles—Ramón and Chris—and brother Reies, Jr. The rest of the 18 were arrested at home and at work, leaving many large families unattended.

Gruesome details of Salazar's murder filled the papers, and were pounded out hourly on radio and TV.

A jailer at the Tierra Amarilla courthouse for 13 years, the 56-year old Salazar lived nearby. He had gone home to supper that night, but left to return to the courthouse, telling his wife he would be back later to take her to a wake. Mrs. Casilda Salazar said that shortly after eight she looked out a window and saw her husband arrive at their front driveway, but in a few minutes the car lights backed away. In the dark she did not see the large patches of blood splattered on the snow, nor the jailer's hat lying nearby.

At eight the next morning, she called Undersheriff Dan Rivera at home and told him, "Eulogio didn't come home last night. I think something has happened to him." Mrs. Salazar had found his hat and the blood. Salazar's car was located about noon, in a snowbank a few miles west of Tierra Amarilla, his brutally beaten body inside.

Experts said there must have been at least three killers, and rewards for information leading to their discovery were offered by TV Station KOB and by private sources.

On Monday January 8, Chicano leader "Corky" Gonzales again came down from Denver to help. Driving his own car to Santa Fe to attend a Supreme Court hearing on the bond revocation issue, he was held in Táos for seven hours on "suspicion of car theft," and thus prevented from getting to Santa Fe in time. He didn't miss much. The courtroom had been packed with FBI men and detectives, and no Alianza supporters were allowed in.

Gonzales went on to Albuquerque, and later reported, "It was much different this time than when Reies Tijerina and his people were placed in jail last June. At that time no one was answering the Alianza phone, the office was closed, people were fearful. Now, the office was open, women were cooking for all the people and guests. People were alive with confidence and enthusiasm. Everyone talked freely . . . . A crowd turned out to the High School auditorium and enjoyed a play sponsored, produced and enacted by the Alianza membership . . . then returned to the Alianza building where they prayed and sang for Reies Tijerina and his people."[7]

The Supreme Court hearing had come as a result of a petition filed by Alianza lawyers. It deposed that the real reason for the wholesale and arbitrary arrests was a public hysteria whipped up by the authorities. They expressed fear that "our state will become known as a totalitarian enclave," and argued that the bond revocation was "a naked exercise of judicial power and without any basis in fact."

Alfonso Sanchez admitted that he had "no direct proof that any Alianzans were involved in the murder," and that no charges in connection with it were pending against any of the 18 being held.

On the same day, the governor attended Salazar's funeral. High ranking politicians, the American Legion, Anglo ranchers and others who would not have given the small-town jailer the time of day, turned out and were solemnly photographed for the press.

Meanwhile, the 18 Alianza members remained in the penitentiary. Governor David Cargo received telegrams from Black and Chicano leaders protesting the incarceration of the land-grant leader and his followers.

H. Rap Brown, national chairman of the Student Non-Violent Coordinating Committee, wired: "We strongly protest the attempt at political assassination of the Alianza . . . and the climate of mass hysteria and attempted destruction of a fellow movement for human rights."[8]

Bert Corona, president of the Mexican American Political Association of California, and Rodolfo Gonzales, president of the Crusade for Justice, also wired their protest.

The wide support for the Alianza, indicating the degree to which the movement had become a symbol of the cause of "La Raza" in the Southwest, startled many New Mexicans.

A week later, the Court ordered 14 Alianzistas released on bond, but directed that Tijerina, Juan Valdez, Tobías Leyba and Baltazar Apodaca be held without bail. Hanging over these four was the capital charge of kidnapping. But even the 14 were not freed. Sheriff Naranjo "went fishing," so that bail could not be posted, while Sanchez filed a new charge against all 20 defendants—assault with intent to kill State Policeman Juan Santistevan. Sanchez contended that Santistevan had been shot at, but not hit, in the courthouse six months earlier. The DA then went to Judge Scarborough, who was to be a witness against the Alianza. He increased bail to $10,000 cash. Bail at this level was far beyond the reach of the accused. The prisoners began a hunger strike, and their families decided to tackle the governor.

María Escobar,* a woman of great moral strength, arrived in Santa Fe to join the confrontation. She had learned that her daughter Rose, in the penitentiary and ill, was on the hunger strike. Rachel Tijerina, 14, and Noë, then about nine, were with her. They had driven from Denver in an old Rambler station wagon laden with family possessions, a large mattress tied on top.

Rachel and Noë had come equipped with Magic Markers, and spent the evening before they saw the Governor producing signs: "Let My Father Out of Prison," "*Justicia para la Alianza,*" "District Attorney Sanchez: Who Will Feed Our Children Now?"

"That Sanchez, he's just like the devil," remarked Noë as he worked. "Not *like* the devil, he *is* the devil," corrected his sister.

Old Santa Fe had a new capitol building, and there the families of the 20 gathered from all over the state early Saturday morning. They waited for Governor Cargo, determined to sit on the luxurious new carpet that covered the lobby outside his office all weekend if necessary.

Cargo's secretary could be seen through the glass doors of the reception room, phone in one hand, counting the crowd with the index finger of the other.

"She'd better tell her boss there's a lot of us, and we're mad," said Mrs. Ezequiel Dominguez. They held the Governor responsible for their predicament because of an impulsive

---

* Reies' first wife resumed her maiden name after their divorce.

remark he had made linking the Alianza with Salazar's death when he first heard the news.

"Governor, you got us into this mess, now you can get us out," Mrs. Tobías Leyba told him when he eventually appeared.

"Ten thousand dollars bail, we can't afford that," said Mrs. Escobar. "In the public eye you have convicted the whole Alianza without any evidence."

"Mrs. Escobar, did you bring Danny back from Denver with you?" asked the Governor.

"What for, she already has two children in jail," Isabel García interjected. She continued, "You know the Alianza didn't have anything to do with this crime, this is the sheep pens all over again."

The Governor sat under a huge wood carving of the State seal, which shows a big, benevolent U.S. eagle with an infant Mexican eagle under its wing.

"Did you know Mr. Salazar? His murder was a terrible thing," he said.

"We don't condone murder," Mrs. García answered. "Nobody wants the murderers found more than we do."

"I don't have the power to reduce the bail," Cargo protested. "That's Al Sanchez' job."

"The raid happened because of Al Sanchez. He is the one that started this persecution of Reies."

"Well, I didn't elect Sanchez," said the Republican Governor. (The District Attorney is a Democrat.)

The Governor took some large photographs of Salazar's bloody corpse out of a drawer and passed them around.

"Tijerina fights for the land but we don't kill anybody," said the brother of Tobías Leyba, who lives near Tierra Amarilla. "Do they have to be blamed because Eulogio was killed? When a jailer stays in office too long you don't know how many enemies he had."

The case against Tijerina had needed a little something extra—murder—to rouse public hatred and set the atmosphere for the trial.

At the beginning of February 1968, Tijerina was freed from the penitentiary. A week-long preliminary hearing resulted in charges being dropped against nine of the Tierra Amarilla twenty. The rest were released on bond. In addition to Reies, the eleven now bound over for trial included his son, Reies Hugh (David), 18; Moisés Morales, 20; Baltazar Martincz, 21; Juan Valdez, 29; Salomon Velasquez, 37; Jerry Noll, 40; José Madríl, 41; Ezequiel Dominguez, 45; and Tobías Leyba, 50.

Tijerina talked with reporters outside the prison: "We're going to organize harder, work harder, and sacrifice more to expose the federal conspiracy against the land-grant villages." He verified reports that he was planning a West Coast fundraising tour, "and we have invitations from New York, Washington and San Antonio."

A tour of California campuses followed, and in March he spoke at the Los Angeles Sports Arena, at a rally of Black Power leaders. "The brown and the black are here tonight to fight the same enemy," he declared, "and this enemy, the United States Government, is trying to oppress the whole world."

Early that spring, he met with Dr. Martin Luther King in Atlanta and joined a committee of 100 delegates to draw up plans for the Poor Peoples' March.

10. Poverty in New Mexico

FOLLOWING THE Tierra Amarilla Courthouse raid, the painful condition of Indo-Hispanos in northern New Mexico was reported throughout the nation, and headlines stressed the failure of the government to give help.

Now a commission of distinguished citizens startled the nation with a report, *Hunger USA,* that showed 256 counties where malnutrition and severe hunger are chronic. Six of the emergency counties are in New Mexico.

Poverty was not new in New Mexico. No one was surprised to hear that "shocking hunger" was endemic in these counties, four of them in the North, where the grazing land is almost gone, and with it the cattle that once supplied meat and whole milk. Anemic mothers sorrowed over infants who died at a rate three times the national average; school nurses noted *resecos,* dry patches on the skin of little children caused by malnutrition; and doctors reported the third highest incidence of rheumatic heart disease in the nation, a consequence of unattended strep infections.[1]

The people who abandoned their villages for Albuquerque were not much better off. There, where 90 per cent of the poor have Spanish surnames, at least 23,000 persons were eligible for food stamps, and there was no food stamp plan.[2]

The six counties named by the Citizens Board of Inquiry have a majority of Mexican Americans, bearing out the government's discovery that "The areas of greatest concentration of low income coincide with those of high density of Spanish surnames."[4]

In Río Arriba, a county the size of Connecticut, two-thirds of the people are of Indo-Hispanic descent. Here 74 per cent have no flush toilets, 70 per cent have no electric or gas stoves, 66 per cent no TV, and 87 per cent have no phone. One-half are on relief.

In 1968, when the national unemployment rate was officially 3.3 per cent, it was 28 per cent in Río Arriba, and those who worked on ranches, that is, most of the Indo-Hispanos, earned an average of $805 a year.[5]

Small farmers in every section of the United States today survive only through unremitting struggle, and often sink beneath the encumbrance of a mortgage. But even inadequate government loans are not available to the northern New Mexico farmer, who certainly fits the requirement that he be unable to obtain credit elsewhere.[6] He is disqualified by "faulty" titles.

"Clear" titles are expensive, and often impossible to obtain. An attorney or abstractor must be hired to trace titles dating back hundreds of years. A condensed history, consisting of a summary of the various links in the chain of title, must be prepared. Finding a trustworthy abstractor is doubtful, and the fee is beyond the reach of a poor farmer. Moreover, the appalling experiences of his neighbors cause him to fear that if he becomes entangled in the web of title search, he may be tricked out of his land altogether.

Herbert C. Little, real estate loan officer for the Farmers Home Administration, complains that the problem of acquiring deeds holds up loans. On the basis of the number of farms and substandard dwellings in New Mexico, the State FHA should rank among the top 15 in loans. Instead, it ranks 38th among 40 FHA lending offices in the nation, with only two offices doing less business. The faulty title problem became permanent, says Little, when the courts established that title would be determined on the basis of U.S. Geological Survey maps that skipped all the Spanish land grants.

On April 1, 1968, as Tijerina was preparing to assume New Mexico leadership of the Poor Peoples' March, Governor David Cargo met with a group of middle-class people in Los Alamos, urging them to "organize a few things" to fight poverty.[7]

Cargo said that he had made 52 trips to community meetings among the Spanish poor in the North, and was "struck by the hopelessness of the situation." One problem, he said, is "obtaining fresh water. In small villages it is normal for people to drink from drainage ditches or from contaminated streams."

He mentioned the "extraordinarily high percentage of New Mexicans from rural, Spanish-American families who have died in Vietnam, because they're the ones drafted."

"Only one of four students in Táos and Río Arriba coun-

ties and only one of six in Mora County complete high
school, and 58 per cent of the people in these counties have a
family income of less than $3,000 a year." While some Federal
poverty programs have been beneficial, some have been "una-
dulterated baloney," he said. The people have "just lost all
faith in government."

Why couldn't Cargo propose a program to revive the economy of the northern counties? Because in the starvation areas,
vast acreages are in the hands of the Federal government. The
counties mentioned by the Governor are in the heart of the
land grants, and anyone who even scratched the surface of the
problem found the reason to be the same: the alienation of
the land.

Two midwest professors who studied Río Arriba and Táos
counties found "starvation amidst plenty; ranchers badly in
need of more stock and of more grazing land for the stock
they have, while not far away is good, ungrazed land, 59 percent of it in the hands of the Forest Service."[8]

Marquis Childs, writing about chronic hunger, also saw the
land at the root of the problem. He warned that the policies
of the Department of Agriculture are a "prescription for disaster." Farm laborers are forced onto relief, and in the hunger
counties relief is deliberately kept down to compel the dispossessed to leave.

"Only a radical system of land tenure and land use, written
into a broad Federal statute, could bring sufficient change,"
he continued. "And any candidate proposing such a radical
goal would have to write off delegate votes in the powerful agricultural states, and particularly in the South and Southwest."

Referring to what Tijerina has often called a conspiracy
against the poor, Childs described "a kind of interlocking di-
rectorate between the officials of the vast bureaucracy of the
Agriculture Department and the Congressional committees
controlling policy and appropriations for Agriculture. . . . For
the big operators it is a highly profitable arrangement."[9]

It is this "vast bureaucracy" that Governor Cargo feared to touch. And although he was distressed by the sight of people drinking from drainage ditches, a basic solution to the problem of water was also beyond his courage to tackle.

That Spring, members of Congress from the Southwest hailed passage by the House of the Colorado River Basin project, to bring more water to the area, a long step toward solution of the region's growing water problem.[10] But Northwest forces, led by Senator Henry M. Jackson of Washington defeated the measure. Jackson acted for the huge power interests of his State, who feared that the project would result in diversion of Columbia River water to the Southwest. Once again, the needs of Mexican Americans were sacrificed.

TIJERINA TALKS BACK

WHY WAS the existence of hunger in New Mexico known to so few outside the State? Until Tijerina and the authors of *Hunger USA* made headlines, and before the Poor Peoples' March, thousands of visitors had traveled through the area, drawn by its tourist attractions, but ignorant of its suffering.

Poverty in the Southwest "has characteristics that are unique in the national American scene," said a panel studying the subject in Arizona.[11] They pointed out that the great distances mask poverty in the rural areas, in the mountains and deserts. Their report spoke of Mexican-American families subsisting on beans and corn, "trying to maintain existence on the fringe of an affluent but hostile society," where the original occupant is barred by racial, social and economic discrimination from participation in the spread of technology and growth of business and industry, and where a "Southwestern power elite of mining, oil, cattle, real estate and agricultural interests tends to sweep social problems under the rug."

It was as spokesman for those who hoped to sweep Tijerina under the rug, that the Albuquerque *Journal* wrote that he

Jane Lougee
Baltazar Martinez

Rose Tijerina at Supreme Court
Building during Poor Peoples' March.

Juan Valdez

was "the wrong choice for leader of the Poor Peoples' March."

And it was rage at the conditions he had known for a lifetime that fired Tijerina's anger when he talked back in a letter published in the *Journal,* May 1, and here slightly abbreviated:

"As Chairman of the Poor Peoples' March in New Mexico, I would like to speak in behalf of the poor people, and also in behalf of my reputation. . . .

"First of all, I feel that to know the poor people, one must know the reasons for the poverty in which they live. . . .

"It is true that I am in trouble with the establishment, and with the enemies of the poor who are in power. But I am also proud to be in this position because of the poor. My reputation is not as bad as the reputation of our government throughout the whole world.

"Besides, for the poor I am more than ready to get in trouble. No poor man can accuse me of fooling him, lying, taking his land, violating international treaties, such as the Treaty of Guadalupe Hidalgo, or burning and destroying the documents and records of Spanish and Indian *pueblos.* . . .

"I cannot be accused of raping and attacking the culture and national characteristics of any people . . . nor can I be accused of converting justice into state welfare powdered milk.

"No poor man, Indian, black, or Spanish American, can accuse me of violence except those with the nature of Senator Montoya, who prides himself in comparing his powers and success with the poor and the oppressed in the Northern part of New Mexico.

"Dr. Martin Luther King knew well the conditions of New Mexico, as well as the conditions of all poor people throughout the world. As for Dr. King appointing me to represent not only the Spanish American poor of New Mexico, but all Spanish Americans throughout the whole Southwest, four witnesses were present in the Chicago International Airport when Dr. King, talking to me, said 'Mr. Tijerina, I commend you for what you are doing in New Mexico for your people.'

"So . . . I am taking part in the poor peoples' march because from the beginning it was I who began the coalition philosophy between the brown and the black people and the Indian people and the good whites. So the fact that the Indians and Spanish Americans are taking part in the poor peoples' march in Washington is proof that I've been interested in unity of all people and justice for all people.

"If Rev. Ralph Abernathy is to honor New Mexico and Albuquerque with his presence May 11, it is because I, 'Tijerina, the Wrong Choice,' invited him personally in exchange for his invitation to me to be in Memphis May 1 at the motel where Dr. King was assassinated, to speak there and begin the march with Rev. Abernathy.

"We should not forget that before his death, Dr. Martin Luther King Jr. and the SCLC [Southern Christian Leadership Conference] were continually attacked by the press and the establishment throughout the South in the same way I have been attacked here."

The *Journal* editorial reflected powerful forces that feared Reies' achieving national prominence. One of these was Senator Montoya, who appeared at a hearing early in April. He didn't believe poverty programs could be handled from Washington, he said. The hearing was attended by members of several Mexican-American community organizations and welfare recipients, who demanded a say in disposition of welfare funds. It took place in the Federal Building in Albuquerque, and outside were Reies Tijerina's daughter, Rose, and a group of picketers. They carried signs calling Montoya "Judas" and protesting the number of Spanish Americans who have died in Vietnam.

On April 26, two days after Rev. Abernathy named him Southwest Coordinator and two hours before he was to leave for Washington, Reies was arrested.

He and 12 Alianza members were held on a renewal of the same charge of first-degree kidnapping, a capital offense, that had been thrown out by District Judge Joe Angel as not sustained by the evidence of 50 witnesses. These new warrants were issued by District Judge Samuel Montoya, first cousin of the Senator. It appeared that a Río Arriba County grand jury had returned secret indictments two weeks earlier.

District Attorney Sanchez said reports that Reies Tijerina and members of the Alianza were arrested to harass the Poor Peoples' March were absolutely false. But Tijerina declared:

"Sanchez refused to comply with Judge Angel's order, and resorted to the Democratic political machine to form a grand jury to prosecute. I feel that Senator Montoya is behind the whole conspiracy. It was well timed. We were arrested a few hours before I was to leave for Washington where I was to meet with Rev. Abernathy. . . .

"I, like all my people, am very much suspicious of the combination of my arrest and the Albuquerque *Journal's* editorial attack on me because I was elected to lead the Poor Peoples' March on Washington. The bonds set against us amount to nearly one quarter of a million dollars. This shows how the powerful authorities try to bleed the poor."[12]

All week the Alianza headquarters had been a beehive of activity. The building was now being shared by Poor Peoples' March organizers, who were making plans for the rally for Reverend Abernathy, and for a march to Santa Fe that was to follow. There, they were to be joined by Indians from Arizona and New Mexico. Reies' arrest was a blow to these plans. His lawyer, Beverly Axelrod, was at first denied the right to visit her client at the penitentiary, and saw him only after calling the Governor.

A protest was made to Attorney General Ramsey Clark when the Committee of 100 visited him in Washington April 29, some committee members threatening to sit in at the Department of Justice until Tijerina and the others were freed.[13] As a result, the $250,000 bond was lowered, and Reies released May 1 in time to speak at the opening of the campaign in Memphis the following day.

A week later, at a meeting at the Kiwanis Club in Española, District Attorney Alfonso Sanchez, "chief legal officer of Santa Fe, Los Alamos and Río Arriba Counties," announced he was running for reelection. He apologized for a pistol he was wearing under his coat. "I'm sorry I have to wear a gun, but it has become a necessity." It was a needless precaution. The only violence dealt Sanchez by the people of Río Arriba was a sound trouncing at the polls.

11. The Poor Peoples' March

ON A sunny Saturday morning, May 18, a five-mile march of more than a thousand people kicked off the Poor Peoples' Campaign in Albuquerque. "Ages, faiths and races mingled," headlined the *Journal,* in the parade that was joined by Roman Catholic Archbishop James Peter Davis of Santa Fe and his counterpart from Anchorage, Alaska, Archbishop Joseph T. Ryan. The archbishops joined with the Protestant president of the New Mexico Council of Churches, and marched side by side with a number of visiting Indians and with Reies Tijerina.

Rev. Ralph Abernathy and other SCLC leaders walked with them through Albuquerque's ghettos. In one thickly populated area they were greeted by crowds, as well as by the stench from the city's sewage disposal plant that pervades this Mexican community.

At the rally that followed in Old Town Plaza, Rev. Abernathy responded to the militant mood of the day. "If the government won't do something about the problems of the people, the people will rise up and change the government," he said.

The previous evening, Albuquerque's largest auditorium had been filled to hear Reies, who shared the platform with Thomas Banyacya of the Hopi Tribe from Arizona, Mad Bear Anderson from the Tuscarora Indian Nation, Clifford Hill of the Creek Tribe, and Beaman Logan, representing the Seneca Nation. Joan Baez was there, and Marlon Brando had spoken at a fund-raising luncheon that day, so all in all the poor people of Albuquerque defied attempts to stay them, and got off to a rousing start.

DENVER

THE SOUTHWEST delegates afterward looked back on Sunday dinner in Denver's Annunciation Church School as the best meal of the whole trip. There, the Crusade for Justice served all 500 a turkey dinner, and as they ate, they were joined by Black Panther delegates. Their leader, Loren Watson, promised, "We'll stay in Washington until Congress passes some kind of progressive legislation." A reporter asked, "Do you think gains have been made in black-white-Mexican unity?" Watson replied that he believed "appreciable coalitions" were being formed.

A contingent of Mexican militants—Brown Berets and their families—arrived from northern California, and their duffel lined the schoolroom together with the luggage of close to 200 Denverites who were taking the trip.

Tomas Manzanares, 12, of Denver, brought his sleeping bag and a scroll signed by 100 students of Columbine Elementary School. "It is a thrill for us that you are representing us on the March to Washington."

The sun shone on the golden dome of Colorado's mile-high Capitol that afternoon, and its grassy slopes, where unemployed coal miners had converged in the 1930s, were now covered with representatives of the modern poor. These wore

Crusade armbands, Black Panther insignia and the full regalia of Western Plains Indians.

At the rally of 5,000, Corky Gonzales and Reies Tijerina were greeted with fervor, and Fred Carr, Crow Indian of Montana, got cheers when he declared that, "Nobody knows what poor is, like the Indian. Nobody has seen horses starving and dead on their own land. The only reason I grew up is because I am mad. We are united with the Negro, Mexican and white." Rev. Bernard Lafayette, coordinator of the Poor Peoples' March, spoke on behalf of the SCLC. The rally's greatest enthusiasm, here, was for Corky, who had often walked up the long steps to that Capitol building to make demands for his people. It was here two years earlier that he had told 2,000 Mexican Americans why he renounced his salaried post in the War on Poverty, denouncing the stubborn racism of Colorado's state officials.

After Denver, the marchers made stops at Kansas City, St. Louis and Louisville, and in each city they caught a glimpse of the different forms that poverty and oppression take in this immense country.

KANSAS CITY

THE CARAVAN, now swelled to 14 buses carrying 600 Southwesterners, arrived in Kansas City at five Monday morning, grateful to be met by hot coffee from Salvation Army trucks, and friendly people, black and white, to serve it.

It was in Kansas City that Reies and Corky together began a struggle that lasted the entire trip, and continued in Washington. They fought for a distinctive voice within the coalition—a Mexican-American voice. They wanted to explain the peculiar problems of the second largest minority, and they sought to reach not only Congress but the entire nation.

And so the New Mexico delegation "sat in" at Kansas City's Livestock Exposition Hall that morning, while their leaders held out for a place on the list of 17 speakers that in-

Poor Peoples' March—conference at Hawthorne School in Washington, D.C., June 1968. *Left to Right:* Rev. Andrew Young, Reies Tijerina, Rev. Ralph Abernathy, Rodolfo "Corky" Gonzales, Roque Garcia.

Reies Tijerina on Poor Peoples' March, Kansas City, May 1968.

cluded the Mayor. At last word came that an agreement had
been reached. Two of the 17 scheduled to speak at the rally in
a ball park had withdrawn in favor of the visitors.

As Tijerina approached the microphone, his delegation
marched into the ball park—surprised when a brass band
struck up a Mexican tune, and at the applause that greeted
them.

Reies was wearing a red headband in honor of his mother,
a Tejas Indian. Though his throat bothered him after the oratory in Denver the day before, the crowd in the bleachers listened intently as he talked of the victims of treaties broken by
the U.S. government: first the Indian, next the Mexican, and
today the Vietnamese.

Three busloads from Kansas City joined the march that
day.

ST. LOUIS

ST. LOUIS received the poor people's delegates on Monday evening, May 20. "They brought with them an atmosphere of
brotherhood and good feeling," said the St. Louis *Globe-
Democrat.*

After a sumptuous meal served in Forest Park by a committee of black churchwomen, all 800 delegates hurried to Kiel
Auditorium. There, in imposing surroundings, the marchers
listened to three hours of homilies by a series of preachers and
city dignitaries, relieved by the fine singing of a choir and the
down-to-earth remarks of Rev. Fred Shuttlesworth, who had
been in on the planning of the campaign before the assassination of Martin Luther King.

But when the chairman of the St. Louis campaign finance
committee began to read off a long list of contributors, the
delegates, seated together in the center of the auditorium,
grew restive. Their leaders waited 15 minutes, but when the
interminable list continued, Corky Gonzales and Reies Tijerina jumped up and walked out, followed by the entire West-

ern contingent. Mexican, black, Indian and white, together
with Negro militants from St. Louis, they held a caucus in the
lobby. The mood was angry. Two members of the reception
committee rushed out after them.

"Don't you think *we* have any culture to contribute this
evening?" Tijerina asked them. Following some negotiation,
it was agreed that the visitors should be introduced.

The St. Louis audience of about 3,000 then were given the
unexpected treat of hearing an epic poem of the Chicano
struggle, "I am Joaquín," recited by its author, Corky Gonzales.*

Its closing lines are:

> *I am still here!*
> *I have endured in the rugged mountains of our country*
> *I have survived the toils and slavery of the fields*
> *I have existed*
>> *in the* barrios *of the city,*
>> *in the suburbs of bigotry,*
>> *in the mines of social snobbery,*
>> *in the prisons of dejection,*
>> *in the muck of exploitation,*
>> *and in the fierce heat of racial hatred . . .*
> *I SHALL ENDURE!*
> *I WILL ENDURE!*

Next morning, the travelers gathered on the bank of the
Mississippi. The Western leg had been increased by a delegation from Texas, black and Mexican, whose occupation was
"harvesting crops for you to enjoy," as Rev. Eutimio García
from Laredo expressed it, and by black youth from St. Louis.

"This is the day the poor must be accepted into the main-
stream of society," said Tijerina. "They must live good *every*
days as we have here. The people that are now joining us are
our ZULU and CORE brothers, and our brothers from

* Crusade for Justice, 1567 Downing St., Denver, Colorado, 1968.

Texas, and any decisions made on this march are going to be made *together* or not at all. In this caravan we don't want slave buses, and we don't want *contratistas.*"

On leaving St. Louis, the poor people staged a symbolic march that shut down the Eads Bridge, a main interstate traffic span across the Mississippi River. They were now over a thousand, and spread completely across the trafficway, singing and shouting slogans, carrying signs that read *"Viva la Raza," "Tierra O Muerte."* They attracted the attention of hundreds of motorists, whose flow they halted for an hour. The Mississippi had not seen such a crew in years.

An old-timer talked of the place that St. Louis had occupied in the Mexican revolutionary movement, when political refugees from the dictatorship of Porfirio Díaz formed a colony here, and printed a paper edited by Flores Magón called *Regeneración,* smuggled back into Mexico where it played an important part in the revolution. He recalled that Magón had been arrested for opposing the first World War, and died in Leavenworth prison, where, some believed, he was strangled by prison guards.

LOUISVILLE

IN THE racket of grinding gears and air brakes, 19 buses pulled into a narrow street of Louisville's ghetto to discharge their load of tired men, women and children from the Southwest.

"They were an older, more mixed, and poorer looking group than the caravan from the urban centers of the Midwest that had passed through Louisville earlier," said the *Courier-Journal.*

The delegation had been warned of abuse and harassment inflicted on an earlier group while passing through Louisville. The tension in the ghetto could be felt, and in fact it would break before long. A rally against police beatings was going on in the street as the wayfarers alighted.

The people of the Louisville ghetto received the Southwest marchers in a way that was different from their arrivals in Kansas City and St. Louis. Here there were no city dignitaries and no need to demand that their own voices be heard.

For their greeting that evening, the black congregation filled the Baptist church, and applauded as tall, mustached Emiliano "Zapata" Dominguez of Denver marched in at the head of a column, carrying the Mexican flag. Rev. A. D. Williams King, brother of the martyred Martin Luther King, welcomed the marchers:

"Regardless of our color, we all have one problem, poverty, and that is why we are here. Not to beg, but to go tell Washington that we want to get rid of it."

"We have come here united," declared Corky Gonzales. "No fast talking reverend or politician is going to take our platform away. We are going to Washington to collect an overdue bill. It has the head of an Indian on one side, and our blood and sweat on the other.

"We have dented the establishment as we came along, and the politicians that have tried to use the poor as a stepping stone."

Reies Tijerina told the congregation:

"It is the excitement of the march that has kept us going, and we hardly notice how tired we are. Today I thought of the little village that was destroyed in Arizona—seventeen homes of poor people burned to the ground in 1957. It had a store, community center, and a church, all built by farm workers trying to escape from being *peones*. We worked together, and shared everything. After the fires, we asked the law officers to investigate. They would not, because they knew all the white rascals who did it.

"The burning of that village was what changed my life. I put down the Bible and picked up the Constitution. It was there I learned that the cops don't give a hoot for the poor. It was there that I learned that the only thing poor people can depend on is to stay together and fight."

WASHINGTON, D. C.

LATE THE next afternoon, the buses were loaded. Tijerina sat behind the wheel of his white pickup, watching until every delegate had taken his seat. Some criticized Reies for not riding in the bus with the rest, but the pickup, scarcely a more luxurious vehicle than the bus, carried the two-way radio with which Reies kept in touch with SCLC headquarters, and guided the caravan to its stops.

One thing they failed to learn on the radio, though, was that the high point of the campaign, Solidarity Day, scheduled for the following weekend, had been postponed until June 19.

Nine days and seven hours after leaving Santa Fe, they sighted the dome of the Capitol, and Tomás Manzanares of Denver lifted his ocarina in the national anthem.

Feet to the earth again at the Sacred Heart church, they were served supper by supporters from Puerto Rico and Panama, under signs reading, *"Bienvenidos," "Venceremos," "Viva la Raza!"*

They heard that Resurrection City did not have room for them, so Tijerina had a place reserved for the Alianza and the Crusade. They were temporarily housed in the Hawthorne School, below the blackboards on which someone had chalked, "Your land—my land."

Paul and Violet Orr, who once had a school in Táos, offered the use of their school here to the Mexican American and Indian delegates in appreciation of the kindness they had found in New Mexico. They were now running the Hawthorne School, a private high school in southwest Washington, a large, two-story concrete building in the form of a hollow square, built around an auditorium with room for a stage.

Hawthorne being strictly a day school, the building was never intended to be lived in, let alone to shelter 600 people. But Mrs. Orr, surely one of the most resourceful people alive, took Reies and Corky down to the basement and showed them where the new electric stove was installed, and upstairs where the gym had been turned into a men's dorm, and how by setting rows of bunk beds and cots against the book-lined walls, the library was ready for the women.

While some New Mexicans went to work on the construction of living quarters in Resurrection City, and a few moved there when a cottage became vacant, there was never room there for all. So that groups of Indian, Appalachian, California and Texas delegations stayed at Hawthorne, as well as black delegates from New York and some Puerto Ricans.

The main force that bound the New Mexicans together, besides friendship and the comfort of talking Spanish, was Reies Lopez Tijerina and his unwavering leadership. He was intimately *there,* 24 hours a day, writing resolutions at a table in the cafeteria, expounding his latest idea for a confrontation with government officials, always accessible, spirited, driving toward a new target.

Leaders of other delegations came to discuss common actions. Reporters from Mexico and England asked to interview him. Representatives of the United Automobile Workers (UAW) and the National Campaign for Agricultural Democracy sought him out, as did many politicians. His lack of sophistication was his chief strength. In Washington, stamping ground of wheelers and dealers, he did not make deals.

RED AND BROWN

LESS THAN a week after they arrived in Washington, the Mexican American delegates were engaged in a historic exhibition of solidarity with the Indian people, afterward praised by Rev. Abernathy as "the most militant, disciplined, creative demonstration that has taken place in the history of non-violence in this country."

The Indians were urging Supreme Court reconsideration of a decision rendered two days earlier, in the case of the Puyallup Tribe *vs* the State of Washington. It effectively denied Washington State Indians their fishing rights, and left hundreds of Indian families without any income whatever.

Tijerina had observed, when told of this struggle, that for the first time black, brown and red people were joining together to support each other's demands. "We are not only in Washington for food and jobs, we are also here to demand the upholding of treaties."

He readily saw the relationship between the Indians' claims and the New Mexico land struggle. Once again treaties had been violated. By the signing of solemn agreements, most of what is now Washington State was ceded by the Indians to the United States, with the provision that the Indians retain their right to fish.

The State of Washington now argued that the treaties should no longer be recognized, since all Indians are now citizens of the United States and the treaties are old. Tijerina profoundly agreed with the Indians' position that a sacred commitment cannot be diminished by antiquity.

Moreover, here again was a clear link between the question of the treaties and poverty. It was another attempt to deny oppressed minorities the right to survive.

So, led by 100 Indian men and women from every part of the country, the delegation of more than 500 Mexicans climbed the long stairs to the great bronze doors of the U.S. Supreme Court, and as they reached them, the doors were slammed shut.

The crowd made way for the Indian women. Dressed in hand-woven blankets in jewel tones, and new buckskin boots embroidered with bead roses, they beat with their small fists on the massive doors of bronze, two stories high and decorated with allegorical figures in life-size bas relief. They sat down and pounded rhythmically on the locked doors, and men in eagle-feather headdresses sat beside them and drummed. "Open the doors, we want justice," and chanted and prayed.

"Open the doors and let them in," chorused the Mexican and Negro supporters, as the Indian delegates sang their high-pitched, blood-stirring ululating prayers.

A messenger from the judges appeared with the proposal that the Indians alone be admitted. This the Indian delegates refused, saying that they needed the support of their Mexican and black brothers. The singing and drumming continued.

Over a thousand demonstrators now crowded under the marble portico, over which in majestic letters is carved, "Justice, Equality Under the Law."

"Let's draw up a list of all the political prisoners," said Tijerina. The crowd was thickly packed on the steps, but a pen and paper were found, and names shouted across people's heads.

Hours passed and several messages went back and forth before John Davis, Clerk of the Supreme Court, emerged with the proposal that 17 Indians and four other delegates be let in.

Forty Capitol policemen flanked the doors, as the petitioning Indians entered. They were led by Al Bridges of the Nisqually and his daughter, young fisherwoman Suzette. With them went Rev. Ralph Abernathy, Reies Tijerina, Rodolfo Gonzales and the Rev. Elmo Jones, representing Southern poor whites.

The petition Tijerina carried asked the immediate release of all political prisoners and victims of racial injustice, "as proof to the world that the Supreme Court upholds the Bill of Rights." It named the Fort Hood 3, Huey Newton, Dr. Spock, Tijerina and 20 members of the Alianza, Eldridge Cleaver, Morton Sobell and the Houston five, among many others.

While their leaders debated inside, 85 Chicano marshals formed a tight protective barrier on the broad steps. Crusaders, Alianzistas, agricultural workers from Texas and Brown Berets from California locked arms. For three hours they led the crowd singing Mexican and freedom songs.

There was a feeling of gaiety among the delegates, "spurred by a new display of togetherness among the Negroes and Mexicans as well as among the one hundred Indians," said a Washington newspaper. They waved their signs and banners at passing cars while the children played in the cooling water of a fountain on the lower plaza.

Across the street, they were faced by a force of District of Columbia police, also standing in the sun, frustrated by the regulation that forbids District of Columbia police on Supreme Court grounds, infuriated at the sight of poor people relaxing on that hallowed lawn.

The delegation suddenly became aware that two strangers had appeared and lowered the flag in front of the fountain. "This is what we've been waiting for," exclaimed a member of the Tactical Unit Arrest Squad as he buckled the chin strap on his helmet, grabbed his night stick and dashed across the Plaza. Though the police took a young couple from Chicago away in a patrol car, the Mexican security guard stood firm on the steps, and the squad was forced to resume their glaring from a double row on the opposite sidewalk.

The delegation emerged at last and Hank Adams of the Indian Youth Council was first to speak:

"When we got up these stairs this morning the doors were shut. We expected this—the doors were shut on our brother Indians centuries ago. We opened these doors. We told them that the Supreme Court and this nation are on trial. We want the Court to grant a rehearing. But if our nation fails, we, like the fisherman and his daughter present today, declare that we will continue to fish."

Rev. Abernathy added that the action of the Supreme Court was a question of genocide, an attempt to exterminate a whole people. "The weapon of starvation is also used against black people, who do not have money to buy food stamps."

As they began the four-mile march back to Hawthorne and supper, the marchers were surrounded by hundreds of police on foot and on motorcycles. Women and children were told to walk in the center of the column, the Chicano marshals protecting the flanks. But as they crossed First and Independence, the motorcycle police charged into a spot where the youth were waiting for the women and children to catch up. In full view of all, four young men, including 17-year old Danny Tijerina, were beaten with clubs as big as baseball bats. The sight of hefty policemen beating a 17-year-old boy, who lay on the street with his arms twisted behind his back, led Rev. Abernathy to say this was the most brutal show of force he'd seen since Selma.

New "Conspiracy" Charges

Meanwhile, back in New Mexico, District Attorney Alfonso Sanchez was facing serious problems in his bid for reelection. Originally appointed to fill a vacancy, he had lost the support of the Chicano population because he had abused the civil rights of the people in the North. The Anglo ranchers also blamed him, because in spite of efforts to jail Tijerina, that durable adversary was putting his message across in Washington and growing stronger at home.

Suddenly, Sanchez' prospects appeared to brighten. On the anniversary of the Tierra Amarilla raid, he had seized the perfect issue—an accusation that would justify trampling every democratic right at Canjilón, and at the same time restore his prestige with the big ranchers.

"Members of the Alianza are being trained in guerrilla warfare tactics in Communist Cuba and on a ranch near Táos," he charged in a newspaper interview. Not only that, said Sanchez, but "they are importing known Communists from Mexico into the region." Tijerina and his brothers are planning a takeover of northern New Mexico "in the same manner Fidel Castro took over Cuba," Sanchez said.[1]

As evidence, he again produced maps and charts allegedly confiscated at the aborted meeting of the Alianza at Coyote a year earlier, outlining plans to establish the "Republic of San Joaquín" in northern New Mexico.* Sanchez declared this constituted a "grave danger" and added that his motive for revealing reports on Alianza activity was to gain the public's assistance in dealing with it.

Seemingly out of context, the newspapers again described the murder of Salazar, with the sinister comment that the jailer was to have been the State's key witness against Tijerina.

The next day, the *New Mexican* reported that "reactions in Río Arriba County to Sanchez' warnings ranged from 'fantastic' to 'ridiculous' to 'unwarranted.' "

Sanchez countered: "The good people of Táos should look into the threat from the Alianza," and said he hoped no danger existed in that area. This insinuation referred to the ranch near Táos owned by Craig Vincent, veteran supporter of liberal causes, where some children from Mexican slums were enjoying a two-week holiday.

Tijerina answered these new charges with a flat denial. He called the Associated Press from Washington to set the record straight: "The real conspiracy to take over northern New Mexico," he said, "is composed of the bankers and lawyers who are descendants of the Santa Fe Ring."

---

* The same sketches had been used as illustrations in a booklet published by the John Birch Society, supposedly exposing a "Communist Conspiracy" to take over the Southwest.

12. Brown, Black, Red, and White

TIJERINA'S CHIEF object in Washington was to make every branch of government, each resident of the District of Columbia, and if possible, every individual in the country a partisan in the fight to regain the land for its heirs in New Mexico. And beyond that, to enlist support in the struggles for justice for the Indo-Hispanic people: the right to preserve their language, culture, education and human dignity against a domineering majority.

He succeeded in reaching hundreds of thousands through the radio, press, TV and public meetings. Everyone knew Reies and the Alianzistas were in Washington.

Day and night he was absorbed in phone calls, interviews, discussions, the preparation of manifestos, petitions and speeches. The office he set up in a small basement storeroom at Hawthorne was constantly crowded. Wilfredo Sedillo, Alianza Vice President, together with half a dozen other land-grant leaders, answered phones, recruited typists and maintained contact with SCLC headquarters.

At night, Rose Tijerina occupied one of the army bunks that lined the wall. Her younger brother and her fiancé, Fabian Duran, also slept in the basement room, as did Sedillo, Alfredo Duran, Juan Roybal, and others who served as war council and bodyguards.

Reies' single-minded drive for recognition of the land grants meant that a large share of the work of obtaining and preparing food fell on the Crusade delegates. Corky's contingent, in which there was a preponderance of young men, also took responsibility for the security precautions that were vital to insure safety of the marchers who sought shelter under Hawthorne's roof. There were individuals who resented Tijerina's constant struggle to keep the land grants in the limelight, but this did not prevent the Colorado and New Mexico delegations from being united on all main points.

Working shoulder to shoulder at close quarters, the contrast in character between the leaders of the two delegations emerged. Corky was well organized, planning for the needs of every member of his delegation that included the California Brown Berets and other Chicano youth. His detailed attention covered not only their frequent militant actions, their discussions and orientations, but took in every phase of their physical well-being. To Corky, organizing a column of march so that all women and children were protected was the true expression of *"machismo,"* of maleness, and it extended to all women whether they wanted protection or not.

Tijerina, on the other hand, was impulsive. Absorbed in the next move, he eagerly sought to try his ideas out on all who surrounded him, new acquaintances as well as Alianza stalwarts. His delegation sometimes had to run to keep up with him, and he worried little where he ate or when.

In all essentials, however, Reies and Gonzales were one: In their total devotion to the cause of Chicano liberation, and in their hatred of the oppressor. Both men displayed such warmth of character, such vigor and enthusiasm that reporters were compelled to seek synonyms for "dynamic" and "charismatic" to describe them.

NON-VIOLENCE

THE CAMPAIGN gathered impetus, and debates on whether non-violence could survive went on day and night. Those who opposed the SCLC's non-violent position won some adherents from marchers who saw that Congress had no interest in solving their problems. They were further "turned off" by the hostile DC police who assaulted them at every opportunity.

Corky expressed this mood at a rally following the Supreme Court confrontation: "America, America, the eyes of the world are watching, your sins are now exposed . . . your numbness to the needs of the poor. Pay your debt in social justice or pay the price in blood."

At the same meeting, held in the AME Zion Church, Reies' favorite parable of the cricket in the ear of the lion got thunderous applause. The great lion, scratching, bleeds to death trying to get rid of the tiny cricket.

This was rhetorical "blood," a kind of safety valve for the people's anger. Long years of frustration burst forth as the villagers from northern New Mexico helped make the church resound: "Black Power! Chicano Power! Indian Power!"

If a member of Tijerina's delegation had seriously proposed violence, Reies would have told him to leave that to the enemy. "Only with justice and righteousness on our side can we win."

Not all the Alianza members stayed for the whole campaign. There was, in fact, considerable coming and going. Modesta Martinez of Tierra Amarilla was there longest, and prominent among the delegates was Pedro Archuleta, founder of Los Comancheros, the youth branch of the Alianza in Río Arriba County. Mrs. Gregoria Aguilar was there, too. She had been penned in the sheep corral at Canjilón, and was first president of the Agricultural Cooperative at Tierra Amarilla.

A dozen carloads arrived in Washington, bringing workers to spend their vacation in support of Reies. And, debating tactics by the hour, were 15 or so dispossessed old men, heirs to disputed grants, who bloomed during the weeks of three unaccustomed meals a day. For, just as the residents of Resurrection City maintained that conditions considered "deplorable" by tourists were better than at home—"Not a rat nor a roach in Resurrection City"—so the meals put together by resourceful Crusaders were superior to the usual diet of these old people from New Mexico, where there is no old age pension. The warmth of communal living and daily meetings also stimulated them; many would have stayed on indefinitely.

Tijerina himself made only one trip out of Washington—to the Conference of Traditional Indians in Oklahoma, invited by Mad Bear (Wallace Anderson) , ship's bosun and leader of the Iroquois League of Six Nations.

He consulted often with Indian leader Al Bridges, and with Cornelius Gibbons, a black leader from New Jersey; Rev. Nieto of San Antonio, Texas; the leaders of the Appalachian delegation, and Father Groppi. Also close to Reies during the Campaign was Richard Romo from the California Peace and Freedom Party.

The chief financial prop of the coalition was a trade union committee in which the UAW was prominent. Corky Gonzales also raised food money from the Catholic Archdiocese and from a united Protestant church committee.

BLACK AND BROWN

FOR THE Alianzistas, one of the most valuable experiences of the campaign was being in action together with black people in a relationship of mutual help. In all of Río Arriba County, the tiny handful of black people who have lived there have in the main been lumber workers brought in by contractors from Texas to divide labor in the local lumber enterprises. Because local people have been denied upgrading in these enterprises, bitterness against blacks has flared up upon occasion. For many people, the distorted presentation by movie, television and press media is their only picture of black people.

When Tijerina invited the late SNCC program director, Ralph Featherstone, and others to the Alianza Convention of 1967, he was criticized by some of his members. They feared that association with black militants would create divisions and precipitate attacks by sections of the Spanish American middle class. It did, and a few withdrew, but Tijerina, whose own position at first was unclear, had become convinced that the Mexicans' struggle could only be strengthened by alliance in brotherhood with the most experienced fighters for freedom in the country. He sought to educate his members, quoting black leaders in his speeches. And here in Washington, Chicanos could see the endurance and wisdom won by the black man's long years of struggle.

Late on a drizzly night, about 50 New Mexicans sat on the cement railing in front of the State Department, when a bus drew up, and out jumped several of Milwaukee's NAACP Commandos in waterproof battle jackets.

"What, no hot coffee? No blankets?" they exclaimed, getting into the bus again, and a half hour later were back with sandwiches, mattresses, coffee and blankets. They asked what this vigil was all about—what did the New Mexicans want from Dean Rusk? Modesta Martinez, Pete Archuleta and the others explained about the Treaty, and afterward the big men from Wisconsin told how they had marched in Milwaukee against discrimination in housing 269 days in a row. Father Groppi, they said, had taught 500 people how to hold a line, what to do in a crisis, how to be militant and disciplined yet non-violent. Something to think about when they got back to their villages.

The delegates to Dean Rusk learned another lesson, too. The Secretary of State refused to see Reies Lopez Tijerina in the presence of the press. Rusk sent his Madison Avenue-groomed secretary out to tell them that he would see ten Alianzistas, alone. They refused. They wanted the world to know what Rusk had to say to demands that he investigate the Treaty of Guadalupe Hidalgo, and if it was valid, enforce it.

Rusk's secretary lost his cool with the villagers that day and snarled at "you people," and Rusk himself went hurriedly to the hospital for "tests," and from there flew directly to

France. So the delegates learned that those at the highest levels of officialdom were no less afraid to confront the issue of the land grants than were their local *políticos.*

Following Rusk's flight to France, David Braaten in a story reproduced and distributed by the Alianza, wrote:

"If any government agency were to escape the wrath of the Poor Peoples' Campaign, the State Department would seem to have been the likeliest candidate.

"It would take a peculiar genius, one might think, to blame domestic poverty on the diplomats in Foggy Bottom.

"Genius or not, Reies Lopez Tijerina has done just that. . . . Tijerina and his followers claim the land would be theirs—as communities, not as individuals—if the United States lived up to the Treaty of Guadalupe Hidalgo. . . .

"It may yet take a Philadelphia lawyer to figure out the shifty dealing and double dealing that surrounded the 1848 treaty. But a fair appraisal of the outcome is that the United States, in the language of the day, hornswoggled the Mexicans. . . .

"Despite the violence that brought him headlines, Tijerina in person is an impressively patient, reasonable man. Handsome, of stocky build and medium height, Tijerina is even cordial to newspaper reporters. It's hard to see why. . . .

"One of the weirdest bits of nonsense is the title stuck on him by an imaginative reporter, supposedly translating his name: 'King Tiger.' 'He was just trying to make me look foolish,' said Tijerina.

"The true derivation of his name, he said, is from the Tejas (Texas) Indian tribe. 'Someone tacked on a Spanish ending. Over the years it changed from Tejerina to Tijerina.' "[1]

On the same day, Paul Wieck of the Albuquerque *Journal's* Washington bureau, reported that the land-grant question "has been pushed into the limelight" by Tijerina, and that he had received a good reception from the eastern press. This impelled New Mexico's Congressman Tom Morris to draft a proposal for a Spanish and Mexican Land Grant Commission.

Emilio Dominguez of Denver Crusade for Justice at State Department vigil during Poor Peoples' March.

Indian-Mexican Mission for the Poor Peoples' March, Washington, D.C., July 1968. *Left to right:* Hugh "David" Tijerina, Wilfred Sedillo, Vincent Montoya, "Mad Bear" Anderson, Reies Tijerina, Ernesto Moya.

It was received with something less than enthusiasm in New Mexico's ruling circles. The commission, the *Journal* reported, was "giving rise to false hopes among natives in the state."

"To some," said the paper, "the Morris proposal looks like an effort to ingratiate himself with the large Spanish-speaking population in his district, estimated to be about one-third of the vote."

Nothing came of the Morris bill, and in the elections that fall Morris himself got knocked over by the fire aimed at Johnson.

Tijerina's uncompromising position toward the Johnson administration attracted many delegates, particularly those from the ghettos of the big cities. The poor of New Mexico had no jobs to lose, no ties with the administration. A leadership free from any obligation to a political machine is what the city poor were looking for.

Puerto Ricans from New York's East Harlem began to appear at Hawthorne. They soon arrived in groups, culminating with Puerto Rican Day. The bond of language was also a tie with the Puerto Ricans, and one of Reies most fiery denunciations of U.S. imperialism, delivered in Spanish, received tremendous response from the crowd on that occasion.

Four thousand Puerto Ricans had come from the factories of the East and the industrial towns of the Midwest, riding buses all night. Now from Tijerina they heard about the Treaty of Guadalupe Hidalgo, and sympathized with Mexicans whose land had been stolen, just as theirs was taken over by U.S. armed might. Corky's slogan, *"No más contratistas,"* was applauded too, by a people who knew hard field labor.

The Mexicans for their part were delighted with the spirited entertainment—the music and poetry offered by the "Puerto Rican strangers from an island far away." They wildly clapped when musicians Pepe and Flora Sanchez prefaced their singing with a stirring appeal for unity in the fight for freedom. "We will never let ourselves be divided by color," said Flora.

Afterward, the Puerto Ricans marched out to Arlington and laid a wreath on the fresh grave of Robert Kennedy. Some walked through Resurrection City to embrace their brothers, who leaned over the fence waving and calling, "Unity, brothers, it's the way to go."

The peculiar mission of the Mexican American, Tijerina believes, is that of a bridge that spans the gulf between nations and between the peoples of our own society. In the world arena, he sees the Indo-Hispano as a link with all Spanish America. In an interview with Dr. Galo Plaza, Secretary General of the Organization of American States (at the Pan-American Union, June 20, 1968), Reies referred to Latin Americans as "our brothers in culture and tradition," and continued: "Within thirty years there will be six hundred million people who speak Spanish.* We belong to them, to that root which carries within it the promise of a great future."

He amplified this thought in a program on News Parade— Channel 9, a Washington radio station (June 16, 1968) :

"We have been forced by destiny to adopt two languages; we will be the future ambassadors and envoys to Latin America. At home, I believe that the Southwest is breeding a special kind of people that will bridge the color-gap between black and white. It will be the brown that fills the gap . . . We are the people the Indians call their 'lost brothers.' "

A demand Tijerina made to every relevant body was that the provision of the Treaty guaranteeing cultural rights be enforced: that an executive order be issued giving priority to the Spanish language and culture on all levels in the Southwest.

He placed the question sharply in this radio interview. "A

* UNESCO estimates that the 1985 population of Latin America will be 434,640,000 and of North America 280,379,000.[2]

major point of contention is that we are being deprived of our language which is our cumulative inheritance. Raping a language is worse than the rape of a child. It has a psychological effect that means we must now catch up with the accumulated knowledge of the Anglo in English."

Later in the program, Tijerina was asked: What do you think realistically are your chances to regain the land to which you are entitled?

And he answered, in a voice of great determination: "The United States is running out of time and out of friends. Circumstances will compel our government to come to the conference table."

SOLIDARITY DAY

ON JUNE 5, the Washington *Post* carried an editorial that praised the "Goals for the Poor" outlined by Bayard Rustin. Rustin, who coordinated the 1963 Civil Rights March on Washington, expected to do the same for the Solidarity Day Rally on June 19. The *Post* was obliged to point out, however, that the Rustin demands were nothing new, that they represented a program that "had been discussed and promised, for a decade." He did not oppose the war, and in general represented the Johnson position.

Two days later, the Associated Press reported from New York that Bayard Rustin threatened to quit. The fact was not that Rustin was quitting, but that the Puerto Rican leaders and others in the coalition, including some SCLC leadership, refused to accept him. An emergency meeting was called at Hawthorne, where David Dellinger warned that the peace forces would pull out unless Rustin were replaced. Reies and Corky, both incensed that none of their demands had been included in Rustin's "realistic goals," also threatened a rupture, as did Hank Adams because the Indians' needs had been ignored.

Sterling Tucker of the Urban League was then agreed

upon, and plans for the event proceeded, but not without further problems. As originally announced, the long list of speakers for this rally, the climax of the whole campaign, included no representative of the Indian or Mexican people, and at first left no room for a Puerto Rican representative, nor for a spokeswoman for the Welfare Rights Organization that was playing a substantial role in the coalition.

Tijerina refused to accept these omissions. He had marched in Memphis, arm in arm with Rev. Abernathy, when Mrs. Coretta King launched the poor people on the road to Washington from the balcony where her husband was murdered. Now Reies appealed to her.

Rev. Abernathy then called another meeting. He reported that Mrs. King had told him the delegations felt left out of the "Juneteenth Day" plans,* and there and then it was agreed that a spokesman for each group in the coalition would have a few minutes on the program.

The time allotted these speakers was so short that Reies wrote out his remarks, an unusual procedure for him, since he was accustomed to gather strength and inspiration from his argument, and from his audience. Getting thoughts on cold paper was not easy. Working late into the night in the basement of Hawthorne, he wrote two complete speeches before dictating one that satisfied him: "Poverty and Misery Have United the Poor This Day," delivered at the rally in a shout of anger that shook the sound equipment.

The words came with the speed and force of a machine gun as he accused the United States of "cultural genocide against my people . . . of genocide against the Indians." They both have been deprived, he cried, "of their property, their human rights, and their SOULS have been deactivated by psychologically inhuman treatment.

"My brothers and sisters, at this moment, are being murdered and mutilated by the Texas Rangers. Our children are

---

* Juneteenth March, named for the day, June 19, 1865, when Texas slaves were freed.

arrested and thrown in jail because they walk out of school in defense of their culture and language. The migrant workers are treated like animals without mercy. . . . Our boys are forced to kill and murder in Vietnam."

His voice could be heard over 15,000 heads, down to the waders in the Reflecting Pool. He told once more of the conspiracy to violate the Treaty signed by the United States and Mexico, although "fifteen million Spanish and Indian people depend on this Treaty for their survival.

"Poor people of the world, let us unite against the enemy of life and human respect. In clean conscience we cannot serve this criminal government that protects the rich and convicts the poor. We will fight, we will ask the whole world for help and support to save our language, our land and our brothers!"

The *vivas* of the Latins in the crowd were joined by thousands of blacks. The day was hot, and clergymen who had lately destroyed draft cards in Maryland passed cups of cool water to children from New Mexico.

Summing up five solid hours of speeches the next day, the Washington *Post* (June 20, 1968) singled out Reies' words as proof that the temper of the nation and of the times had shifted in the five years since the first massive civil rights march.

"Yesterday, Reies Lopez Tijerina could accuse the United States of 'organized criminal conspiracy' and 'cultural genocide' against Mexican-Americans," but five years earlier John Lewis, SNCC chairman, "had had to tone down his speech scorching 'cheap politicians.' "

Tijerina and the SCLC

In the brief weeks of the Campaign, Reies' relations with the SCLC underwent three changes. Because he had never been part of a coalition, nor worked with a national organization, he at first tended to expect too much of the SCLC. He did not take into account the severe problems of this nationwide committee of black people in active battle for their liberation. The SCLC failure to consult with other groups before postponing the Solidarity Day Rally, a date agreed upon by the Committee of 100, both he and Corky considered a slap at Mexican leadership.

From boundless faith in the experience and power of the SCLC, Tijerina veered toward disillusion and indignation when the demands of the Chicano were not immediately embraced.

But he responded to the efforts of Rev. Abernathy and the boundless tact and understanding of SCLC vice presidents Coretta King and Andrew Young. He also became aware of the severe pressures the SCLC labored under, not only from racist forces in Washington but from provocateurs within Resurrection City. Thus, by June 19 Reies' focus became clearer and he sharply denied reports that he had split with the black civil rights movement.

Naomi Nover of the Denver *Post* reported June 12 that Tijerina planned to move into Resurrection City in the near future. Asked how things were going in the Poor Peoples' Campaign, Tijerina replied:

"So far, so good, considering the wide scope of the over-all program. For the first time in history—an attempt is being made to organize and unite the poor and find an identity in organized force.

"This Poor Peoples' campaign," Tijerina added, "is a monumental expression of the peoples' struggle to bring the government to a position of direct talks with the poor."

And although a month was too short a time to develop what Tijerina called "the coalition philosophy between the brown people, black people, the Indian people and the good white people," progress had been made. The leaders of the various groups were no longer stung by press reports designed to exploit their smallest difference, and a "new populism" was ripening.

On June 21, two days after Solidarity Day and three days before the destruction of Resurrection City, a meeting of the coalition steering committee took place. In addition to the SCLC leaders, Corky Gonzales and Tijerina, it included such Indian representatives as Hank Adams of the Indian Youth Council, Cliff Hill, chairman of the Cherokee delegation, and Mad Bear. Two young men from Puertorriqueños Marchan were there, as well as National Welfare Rights spokeswomen; Robert Fulcher from Appalachia; Rev. Leo Nieto of Austin, Texas; Mr. Guerro with the National Campaign for Agricultural Democracy; Attorney Beverly Axelrod; a Negro teacher from Beaumont, Texas and a delegate from the Wyoming ranchhands.

The meeting was opened by Rev. Abernathy. He spoke of the difficulties of the Campaign, robbed of its leader without notice, which he described as the "most massive, most complicated movement in the history of the civil rights struggle."

Rev. Bernard Lafayette then introduced the problem presented by the imminent expiration of the permit for Resurrection City. The discussion that followed centered around the possibility of a struggle to save the City. Some felt that, as a symbol to poor people, it should be fought for. There was debate.

Reies expressed the opinion of the Western contingent. He asked for mutual agreement as to just how far each should go in support of the other's demands, in this instance the extension of the permit for the City.

"Some of the groups want to push their issues as far as fight or jail. Are you ready in exchange to go all the way with our issues? We must think how much. I'm ready to go fight or to jail if it is *together*."

Rev. Abernathy replied that he was not "asking anybody to go to jail over this particular issue. It is for the SCLC staff to decide."

Only Mad Bear seemed to foresee the holocaust. He said: "The FBI and Secret Service will do anything they can to see

Resurrection City gone. When they come in with their troops there is going to be hell."

Three days later, Rev. Abernathy was in jail and Resurrection City destroyed.

13. Back in New Mexico

TIJERINA RETURNED to Albuquerque July 20, 1968 to resume the fight at home.

"We have remained in Washington D.C. for 62 days with the Campaign of the Poor. For me it was the greatest experience of my life," he told a crowd of several hundred gathered to meet him at the airport.

"In a few words, the poor have shifted the 'burden of proof' off their shoulders. In the eyes of the world now, the 'burden of proof' is on the rich and no longer on the poor. It is only the poor who have the right to question the rich man about his honesty and his wealth.

"And now we announce that the poor have completed one of the country's greatest missions: to peacefully demand from our government 'equal justice under the law.' "

The Poor Peoples' Coalition, that had been projected in Washington, did not get off the planning board. Most of its components, returning to ghettos and reservations that election year, became involved in local battles.

Reies himself was immediately caught up in the political campaign and in legal motions. In the Tierra Amarilla case, both sides were seeking a change of venue for the trial. DA Sanchez claimed that an impartial jury could not be found in Río Arriba County. The defense countered with a motion that questioned whether Tijerina could receive a fair trial anywhere in New Mexico, in view of Sanchez' lurid stories about the Alianza training men for guerrilla warfare.

PEOPLE'S CONSTITUTIONAL PARTY

WHEN TIJERINA got back to his headquarters, he found a small meeting of non-Alianza community leaders in progress. One of them took him aside and asked, "Reies, why don't you run for Governor?" "Ay! Don't I have enough troubles?" "Yes, but it would be a fine chance to get your ideas across. Think of all the free TV time. Besides, these *vendidos* in the two old parties need shaking up."

In California that fall there had been talk of Tijerina running for vice president on the Peace and Freedom slate, but Reies insisted he would do so only if Dick Gregory headed the ticket. As it turned out, Peace and Freedom did not get on the ballot in New Mexico.

After lengthy discussions with the board of elders, the *Mesa Cósmica,* the Alianza decided to launch an independent Peoples' Constitutional Party *(Partido Constitucional del Pueblo),* and on August 4 held a founding convention. Key to Tijerina's platform was the right to bilingual education and restoration of Indo-Hispanic culture. "I'd enforce that law for bilingual education, even if I had to call out the National Guard to do it," he said.

At the PCP's founding convention Tijerina explained why he was running for office.

"I never wanted anything to do with politics, but this is why I changed my mind. Not only the land has been stolen from the good and humble people, but also their culture and something else very valuable—their vote. I have seen how the bad politicians abuse it.

"Like a single force as one man, the fists of the poor must be united to deal a blow to the enemy. . . . If I am elected, the worker will be honored with a just wage and brakes will be put on the rich."

The PCP held conventions in six countries.* Tijerina was at them all. In San Miguel, where he read the list of local beneficiaries of "rich man's welfare"—big ranchers who in that impoverished county were getting up to $30,000 from the Department of Agriculture for *not* planting crops—he was constantly interrupted by whistles, clapping, laughter and shouts.

He added points to his program: a civilian police review board, investigation of corporations and banks that speculate with the property of the people, ending discrimination in draft boards. He promised to fight for an increase in state welfare checks, and pardon for those convicts who, because of their poverty, had not been adequately defended in court. A final plank called for the 18-year-old vote and protection of the rights of hippies, "and all who want to live their own way of life."

At the University of New Mexico, in a "notably enthusiastic, excited and vigorous speech," Tijerina said that if he were governor, "The poor will have a good time watching the police chase the rich." When asked about the Black Panthers, he said, "They are brave. I want them as my friends."[1]

The Río Arriba County convention was held in the mountain village of Gallinas, on the San Joaquin grant. Three hundred voters squeezed into the dance hall to select their candidates. Seven men and a woman were nominated from the floor and unanimously approved. Tall Pedro Archuleta, Jr., just back from the Poor Peoples' March, smiled shyly as he was picked to run for state representative. White-haired Belarmino Maes stood with dignity to accept nomination as county commissioner, adjusting his suspenders with hands worn by a half century of farming. He said that he had worked for the Democrats all his life and got nothing. "Now we will work for ourselves."

Reies was listened to with attention as he spoke of building a new society, "where man does not exploit his brother."

* Bernalillo, Río Arriba, Santa Fe, Sandoval, Valencia and San Miguel.

A thunderstorm threatened, and the heat grew stifling. The crowd flowed outdoors, and Tijerina, surrounded by the newly chosen county committee, conferred in the back of a pickup, getting organized as the clouds gathered.

The editor of the Santa Fe *New Mexican* devoted a lengthy editorial to Tijerina, quoting freely from the John Birch Society magazine, *American Opinion*. Tijerina was compared to V. I. Lenin, "who first conceived the war on poverty in seizing the government of Russia." The article called the Alianza leader a "Castroite terrorist," and quoted his brother, Ramón Tijerina, as declaring that Che Guevara was not only alive but was in Tierra Amarilla, and that "in 30 or 40 years a vast monument will be built to him there."

Reies responded by challenging his opponents to find the killers of Eulogio Salazar. If elected, he said, he would appropriate $100,000 reward for information leading to the conviction of the murderers, and would bring every available Federal agency into the investigation.

Both Albuquerque dailies attacked Tijerina, who promptly called on the U.S. Attorney General for an anti-trust action against "the newspaper conspiracy of the Albuquerque *Journal* and Albuquerque *Tribune*." In a letter to Attorney General Ramsey Clark, Tijerina said that secret agreements and corporate arrangements between the two papers were a criminal conspiracy against the citizens and people of New Mexico. "Entered into in the 1930s, it has resulted in suppression of news. Specifically, these newspapers either do not cover, or attack editorially, efforts for the benefit of the Indo-Hispano population."

Tijerina stickers and placards were sprouting up in the northern countries, and groups of ladies were driving up from Santa Fe to remove them. It was then that Secretary of State Ernestine Evans knocked off the ballot the names of eight PCP candidates. Mrs. Evans disqualified Tijerina because he had been convicted of interfering with an officer of the Forest Service—a felony in Federal court but only a misdemeanor in

New Mexico. Dr. Roger Anderson, geologist and peace leader running for the Board of Education, was disqualified on a technicality; Preston Monongye, candidate for district attorney, because he was not a member of the bar, and Wilfred Sedillo and Bill Higgs on the pretext of residence requirements. No reason was given for disqualifying the other three.

A hearing was called before the State Supreme Court (October 15, 1968) to direct the Secretary of State either to place PCP candidates on the ballot or "show cause" why she should not. The real issue, understood by all although never stated out loud, was the right of the poor to hold office.

The three-judge court was uncertain about the meaning of "learned in the law," the state constitution requirement for district attorney. Monongye, a Hopi Indian silversmith with 14 years in law enforcement on the Jicarilla Apache Reservation, had studied law by correspondence. Elderly Chief Justice Chavez recalled New Mexico's 1910 Constitutional Convention.

"The man who became Chief Justice Bratton, also Judge Fall of Tennessee, and many of the others that took part in the Convention, never attended law school. I keep wondering if it is Mrs. Evans' prerogative to determine who is learned in the law and who is not."

An attorney for the State replied indignantly, "If the *voters* were to determine who is learned in the law, it would be meaningless."

ACLU Attorney Jonathan Sutin, on the contrary, argued that in relation to Tijerina, "The people of New Mexico have the right to decide. The people in effect will pardon him if they think he is qualified. If a man convicted of a crime cannot run for office while his case is on appeal, it would mean that voters convicted of a crime but whose cases are on appeal cannot vote in this election."

State's Attorney O'Dowd seemed consumed with fear that the government might actually get into the hands of the people. "Somebody has got to stop somewhere. These individuals are not *entitled* to run for office. Everybody's names can't go on the ballot, there is no room on the machines. The money that is going to be expended is astronomical. We took off a Negro candidate 24 years of age.* Would you allow a two-year old to run?"

A judge asked O'Dowd if he had checked on all the Democrats and all the Republicans, and he admitted that he had not. He added: "We were faced with eight minor parties,† and we've eliminated three of them."

Judge: "Because the machines are too small? That doesn't answer the issue."

A week before the elections, the Supreme Court ruled Tijerina off the ballot. The same decision also disqualified Monongye, but the judges held that the Secretary of State erred when she disqualified Sedillo, Higgs and Dr. Anderson, and refused to certify three other candidates.

"It was one of the most far-reaching decisions ever handed down by the court, and its many rulings will affect future elections and future court cases," wrote Wayne S. Scott.[2]

It threw out the State law requiring congressmen to live in the district they represent, and ruled that the candidate of a minor party need not be a registered voter of that party.

The PCP convention was immediately reconvened, and Jose Alfredo Maestas certified to run in Tijerina's place. Stepping into the slot for lieutenant governor was Mrs. Crucita Chavez of Albuquerque.

These events threw the state electoral machinery into a turmoil. The new slate was to be placed on the ballot by means of gummed stickers, but 8,000 absentee ballots had already been sent out, over half of them to New Mexico residents serving in Vietnam.

After the elections, there were complaints of gross irregu-

---

* Peace and Freedom candidate Eldridge Cleaver.
† The Democratic, Republican, American Independent (Wallace) and Socialist Workers parties appeared on the ballot in addition to the PCP.

larities from many counties, and Tijerina filed a formal protest. In Bernalillo County, which contains the city of Albuquerque and nearly a third of the state's population, straight ticket voting levers for the PCP were blocked. Election officials excused this on the ground that the PCP did not have a full slate running, but although only the Democrats put a full slate forward, the PCP alone was blocked. Less than 3,000 votes were tabulated.

The effect of the Peoples' Constitutional Party in the 1968 election, however, went beyond the votes it received. In three statewide races, the candidates were well above the margin of victory for the winner. In 1969 the state legislature passed a new law with stiff requirements that "effectively eliminated all but Democrats and Republicans from the ballot."[3] The PCP filed suit, contending the new law was aimed to disfranchise them, and were successful in having it taken off the books. In 1970 the new party doubled its votes.

First Tierra Amarilla Trial

As the first Tierra Amarilla trial opened, District Judge Paul Larrazolo ruled that he would try Tijerina separately from his nine fellow defendants. Tijerina then announced that in view of this move that deprived him of the aid of the other defendants and their lawyers, he would defend himself. "We worked together for months," he said. The judge gave him the right to act as his own lawyer, but denied him time to prepare. Prosecutor Love argued against any delay. "The State can't wait until they can teach Mr. Tijerina how to try a law case," he sneered. Tijerina was given two hours to prepare for trial of a capital charge. The *Journal* gloated, "The fiery Tijerina, a former Texas cotton picker, is not a lawyer."

But as the trial proceeded, the paper was comparing Tijerina to Clarence Darrow, and at its end quoted a woman juror who said, "The man has a fantastic mind." On the third anniversary of the incident a sheriff's deputy vividly remembered how he had been riddled by Tijerina—on the witness stand.

The night of his acquittal Tijerina said he believed his victory was due to the state's witnesses, who started "a chain reaction of changing their testimony." It was his own bold cross-examination that started their chain reaction. He was charged with kidnapping and false imprisonment of Deputy Sheriff Dan Rivera, and Rivera had said that he was pistol-whipped by Tijerina's orders and in his presence. Yet under Tijerina's daring and persistent probing he admitted that Tijerina had nothing to do with the beating. "I'm not blaming you for anything," he whined.

Close to 50 witnesses testified for Tijerina, and more waited to take the stand; but the judge who had said at the beginning, "I don't intend to let this trial deteriorate into a hearing on the title to land grants," now said he was tired of hearing from the small farmers and their wives who were fighting to save Tijerina.

In his summation, Tijerina declared, "Yes, we are guilty of claiming our lands, and we are guilty of unifying northern New Mexico, guilty of believing in the treaty of Guadalupe Hidalgo," and once more accused the State's witnesses of lying against him "to cover up the great political chain of Río Arriba County."

The State had asked for a first-degree kidnapping conviction that carries a penalty of death in the gas chamber. Alfonso Sanchez ended his closing statement with the plea: "I implore you to find this man guilty of first-degree kidnapping. I do not care if you recommend life imprisonment, but the court must have complete jurisdiction over his life."

As he left the courthouse after the verdict, an unseen person shouted from a passing car, "We'll get you yet, Tijerina!" Word spread that the jury had been intimidated by threats from the Alianza, and civil libertarians were shocked when the *Journal* quizzed the jury. The overriding opinion of the jurors, however, was that the State failed to prove its case, and that much of the evidence was in conflict. One juror added that no one had based his verdict on fear. "A lot of people think we did it because we were afraid, but none of us felt that way at all."

Keen Rafferty, respected professor emeritus of journalism at the University, protested the *Journal's* enquiry. "Whatever else may be said, he is a brave man who won his case fair and square against the obvious wishes of the whole commercialized power center in the state."[4]

In an editorial expressing the intent of this "power center," the *Journal* sincerely hoped that the rest of the charges against Tijerina would not be dropped, and recommended the appointment of a special prosecutor to try him again. The editor once more raised the ghost of Salazar and reminded his readers that: "One of the officers who would have been a key witness, later was brutally murdered."[5]

In the meantime, Tijerina's acquittal stunned New Mexico and delighted Mexican Americans all over the Southwest. Congratulations poured in, as well as invitations. Newspapers throughout the Southwest carried feature articles describing his victory.

"New Mexico was in a state of shock after the acquittal," wrote Ed Meagher of the Los Angeles *Times* (December 18, 1968). He quoted an exuberant Tijerina as saying that he first intended to rebuild the Alianza, that once had numbered 8,000 members. Then, said Meagher, Tijerina will involve himself in a suit against the boards of education. Tijerina foresaw a cultural renaissance. "The cultural spirit is on the warpath, he explained. Each race is out to rescue its identity. That's why the Black Panthers."

The Denver *Post,* in a lengthy article (December 29, 1968) commented: "Whatever you think of Tijerina you must concede his importance. You must also concede that his importance is growing." Tijerina's victory, it said, was "a stunning blow to the establishment and opened the door for more confrontations in the state." "We are planning a mass occupation

of the San Joaquín del Río Chama in the spring," Tijerina
told the paper. "We have 200 members of the Alianza already
living there, in the spring we will move in by the thousands."

The Sacramento *Union* (May 10, 1968) reported an omi-
nous warning by the "Zapata of the Southwest"—grapes now,
lands next. Tijerina, at a press conference, declared that
César Chavez' campaign to unionize farm workers "already
has helped everyone in the Southwest." Asked if he felt he
would win out in his struggle to reclaim lands, he answered,
"My question is will the United States survive with all its con-
spiracies?"

VIOLENCE AGAINST ALIANZA

SIX MONTHS of intense activity followed for Tijerina and the
Alianza. In January 1969 the battle for a $3.50 minimum
wage for Albuquerque's garbage men was begun, and on the
19th Tijerina was in Santa Fe urging the Board of Health and
Social Services to raise welfare benefits by 25 per cent and
"treat poor people with more respect, because it is the poor
that cause things to be done." On the same day, he met with
Governor Cargo to request him to deliver his address to the
opening session of the State legislature in Spanish. The Governor agreed to have his speech translated and make copies
available.

In February he addressed students on campuses from Las
Vegas to California, and in early March, an Alianza delegation visited Washington in a continuing struggle to get action
in Congress calling for an investigation into the "legal, political, and diplomatic status of lands which were subject to
grants" from Spain and Mexico prior to the Treaty that
ended the Mexican-American War. They first contacted Representative Manuel Lujan and Senator Montoya, both of New
Mexico, who refused to sponsor the measure. The resolution,
HR 318, was introduced by Representative Henry Gonzalez
of Texas, who is no friend of Tijerina, but thought it was

time the matter was settled. The resolution was referred to the House Rules Committee, and has not been heard of since.

In one week in April he made speeches to such diverse audiences as the members of the National Welfare Rights group of Ratón, a coal mining town on the Colorado border, and the National Lawyers Guild in New York City.

In May an NBC First Tuesday Program devoted to the second largest and "until now most apathetic minority," labeled Tijerina "the most hated man in New Mexico," and told how the "survivors of the Sixteenth Century dream of wealth in the New World, subsist on food stamps." "It's not all that bad," grumbled State Police Chief Joe Black.

As Tijerina's movement gained strength, it aroused such fear and hatred from racist forces that its headquarters were blasted by dynamite twice in two months; a building near Táos burned to the ground five hours after Tijerina announced it would become an Indo-Hispano cultural center; the cooperative clinic about to be opened by Alianza members in Tierra Amarilla was put to the torch; and the small home of a member of the Alianza Supreme Council destroyed by dynamite while his family slept. In March Tijerina's trip to California was cut short by an explosion that damaged the Alianza and endangered the lives of his wife and two little children. The author was sleeping on a cot in the Alianza building during Tijerina's trial in December 1968 when four bullets were fired into the main hall. Police, summoned immediately, arrived eight hours later, looked at the holes in the wall, and left. Tear gas was injected into the vent of a car parked outside the Alianza at a time when the block was covered by police. All of these attacks were viewed by law enforcement officers with casual unconcern. Tijerina's telegrams to Washington demanding an investigation were ignored.

The only man to be held by police had blasted one side of the building a year previously. Fellion, a former sheriff's deputy, blew his own hand off in the act. Charges against him were dropped by Judge James A. Maloney, who was elected

Attorney General in the fall of 1968, and thereupon took charge of prosecuting the Alianza.

The year 1969 began with an invitation to all to attend the sixth anniversary of the Alianza in Albuquerque, on February 2. "In the last six years," said Tijerina in the announcement, "New Mexico has seen a movement that is stronger and has brought more changes than any other. In six short years the Alianza has gained the respect of governors, the Department of Education, the courts and even the bankers. In the six years of the Alianza, more history has been written in defense of the rights of the Indo-Hispano and of the poor, than in the previous hundred years."

The two principal items on the agenda of this convention were the fight for bilingual education and the legal and popular aspects of the occupation of San Joaquín.

LANGUAGE OF THE OPPRESSOR

To TIJERINA, the suppression of the Spanish language was, next to land robbery, the most powerful weapon used by the Anglo to preserve his dominance. He told a symposium sponsored by the United Mexican-American Students at the University of California at Los Angeles (March 1, 1968), "We are angry because they have stolen our lands and language. They gave us the 'freedom' a man gives to a bird in a cage. They took the scissors and clipped both wings (land and language). Language is our freedom—language which is the result of the accumulated centuries—the food left us by our forefathers."

A person who has never been denied the right to speak his own language has difficulty appreciating the deep psychological hurt such deprivation causes. As imperialists long ago discovered, forcing a man to speak the language of the conqueror keeps him at a disadvantage, and serves to maintain and emphasize the master-servant relationship. When one is obliged to express himself in a foreign language, shades of meaning are lost; the speaker fears that a mispronounced word may trap him by becoming ridiculous or obscene.

In the Southwest, children are punished for talking Spanish at school, even at recess. Those who are not proficient in English are often classified as "retarded," and Anglo students cannot help but be impressed with their own superiority when they pass a classroom filled with "backward" Mexican children, who have been proven to do well when tested in Spanish and may often be contributing to the support of their families.

Discouraged and humiliated, Chicano youth are "pushed out" of school in large numbers. According to the U.S. Office of Education, the result of the suppression of languages native to the region is that "Mexican-Americans and Indians in the Southwest are the most educationally retarded groups in the country, with an average attainment of less than eight grades. The average Negro reaches a ninth grade level, while the average attainment of the Anglo is the 12th grade." The report omitted to say that for Indians the average grade level is only the fifth.

Many educators have used the saying, "illiterate in two languages" to describe students of Mexican descent. This, says a northern New Mexico paper, "is an absurd statement because these so called ignorant students are capable of communicating with over 130 million Spanish speakers who populate the Hispanic world from Northern Michigan to Southwestern Argentina and from the Philippine Islands to Spain."[6]

Tijerina says, "Spanish I use 98 percent of my time. Two percent of my time I speak this language. I was speaking to 500 people and one Anglo came proudful to the platform and says, 'Hey, talk English so I can understand you.' I told him 'you go to school and learn Spanish just like I learned your language.' "

Although he hated the English language as an instrument of oppression, Reies concluded that he needed to master it in order to bring the message of his struggle to wider audiences. He undertook this task with vigor and frankness, good humoredly cursing the unwieldly idiom and asking for help in achieving clearer formulations as he went along. An early speech in English was delivered with difficulty in 1966, but by the time he argued his own defense at the December 1968 trial a remarkable advance had been made in his command of the unfriendly tongue—a fact sarcastically commented upon by prosecuting attorneys every time Reies apologized for his lack of facility.

As soon as the December trial was over, Tijerina appeared at the Albuquerque Board of Education to demand sweeping changes in the school system. In an appeal on behalf of those "who have been most poorly educated," Tijerina submitted a list of 12 proposals to guarantee equality in the school system, an important step toward equality in jobs.

"Tijerina launched into the oratory which has brought him fame," reported Rees Lloyd. He charged that "our children have been controlled, terrorized and inferiorized by the Board's tactics." He scourged the Board as part of a conspiracy to "deprive our people of their life, spirit, and heritage," of "thrusting the children into a melting pot intended to melt them white."[7]

The Board adjourned immediately after Tijerina's fiery words, ignoring the Alianza's proposals. These included teaching Spanish as the primary language in some schools, an end to unfair practices in hiring Indo-Hispano teachers, community control of schools, and discontinuance of the system whereby poor, Indo-Hispano children are placed in slow groups, white children in fast, college-bound groups. The proposals stressed the need for a reorientation of history courses now taught from an exclusively English viewpoint,* toward a "great increase in the teaching of Spanish and Mexican his-

---

* Children in Southwest schools are taught that the war against Mexico began when Mexico invaded the United States.

tory, heritage and culture through literature and other artistic and popular forms."

The following week the Alianza filed suits against the Boards of Education of several cities, including Albuquerque. The charges detailed discrimination against specific children of 20 Alianza families, including Tijerina's own. They formed a large group, and crowded into Albuquerque's Federal Building to file the suit that attacked the constitutionality of New Mexico school laws. The suit was dismissed a year later, and the appeal turned down by the U.S. Supreme Court in the spring of 1970 with only one dissenting vote, that of Justice Douglas.

The suit would have reestablished the position of State supervisor of Spanish instruction in New Mexico and required teaching of Spanish in the public schools. Tijerina and the Alianza asserted that repeal of these measures in 1967 unconstitutionally discriminated against Spanish-speaking children, and that their revocation was designed to destroy knowledge of Indo-Hispano history, language and culture.

On the same day that the Supreme Court denied the Alianza repeal, the U.S. Department of Health, Education and Welfare notified more than a thousand school districts that they must remove language barriers which handicap Spanish-surnamed pupils! These Southwestern districts were warned that they must not assign non-English-speaking students to classes for the mentally retarded, or deny them access to college preparatory courses, or they would face loss of federal funds under the provisions of the Civil Rights Act of 1964.

This directive caused school boards in several counties to reexamine their practices. In some schools, Spanish classes were instituted in the lower grades, and in others a cursory reference to the history of the Mexican people was included in high school classes.

The Las Vegas (N.M.) Board of Education heard its lawyer declare, "That suit that Reies Tijerina filed is one of the most dangerous suits ever filed against the Board of Education," and Tijerina told an Alianza gathering that "from California, Texas, and all over they are congratulating us."

To dramatize the campaign against the suppression of Spanish, the Alianza held a parade through Albuquerque on May 17, 1969. The celebration commemorated the 429th anniversary of the Spanish language in New Mexico, and drew more Alianzistas than ever before. Young men from the North rode their prettiest horses and land-grants families marched in colorful costume.

Homemade floats stretched for more than ten blocks, bearing such signs as "I Speak Two Languages, Do YOU?" and "In 2000 AD there will be 600 million Indo-Hispano people." Shoppers and workers came out on the sidewalk to wave and cheer, and Reies looked delighted with his children, in *charro* (Mexican cowboy) costume. The two-hours march ended in Old Town Plaza with a rally that featured a double mock wedding, marking the date on which Spain in 1540 authorized marriages between Indians and Spaniards, to found the "Indo-Hispanic race." An Indian man from San Ildefonso Pueblo was joined in symbolic union with a Spanish woman, while Rosario, a Spanish man, was united with Genoveva from Acomita Pueblo.

The original proclamation and ceremony were read by Father Leonard Baca, but current struggles were the topic of the speeches that followed. Clemencia Martinez, Welfare Rights leader, declared that "They want us to get off welfare and work. Then they should pay us the same as the white man. Ask them, how many Mexicans does the telephone company employ?"

Students from the University of New Mexico spoke from the painted bandstand. "There is injustice at the University. Janitors and other workers are Chicano, except for the supervisors. They have not been allowed a union, and are receiving less than the minimum wage."

Mexican music and an art display attracted a large crowd. Reies made one of his most impassioned speeches.

"Men and women must be free from birth to develop all their rights, political and cultural. That is the only thing that can bring satisfaction and joy to being a resident of the United States. The educational system in New Mexico is part of a conspiracy against our rights. They want to keep our heritage secret from us, like a stepfather that spends the inheritance of a child and keeps him in rags." Briefly translating his remarks into English, he advised his listeners to "remember, the English speaking are a minority on this continent."

At the dance in the Alianza hall that evening, the floor was crowded with "*valientes*"* and their wives, all eager to show their skill at *La Raspa*† and the polkas and varsoviankas of their grandfather's days, climaxing with a local favorite, "La Indita."‡

14. Tijerina Tried Again

IN APRIL, the Alianza invited all who wished, to move onto the San Joaquín grant. "We decided to squat on Forest Service land so that the government would have to prove their ownership in order to kick us out. But the government prepared a criminal ambush," said Tijerina later. From Coyote, Mayor Jose Lorenzo Salazar had served notice on the Governor and Chief of Police that any attempt to harass settlers would be met with citizens' arrest.

The *New Mexican* (April 8, 1969) responded with an editorial urging the Federal government to be firm in "protect-

---

* The Brave—Tijerina's name for the Tierra Amarilla defendants.
† Known to folk dancers as "Put Your Little Foot."
‡ "The Little Indian Woman."

ing public property." Two years ago, Tijerina and a group of followers had taken over Echo Amphitheater in the same area, it warned, and "other incidents of violence have occurred, including an armed raid by Tijerina and a band of his followers on the Río Arriba County Courthouse, and a *subsequent brutal murder of a courthouse jailer.*"

After the Spanish Day parade, Tijerina and Patsy, together with two-year old Isabel and baby Joaquín (named after the grant) moved a trailer up to Coyote, and Reies held a series of popular rallies, culminating with an encampment on the second anniversary of the events at the Tierra Amarilla Courthouse.

Visitors from all over the Southwest, and some from Chicago and New York, pitched their tents and spent the weekend with hundreds of grantees and their families. Youthful Brown Berets from Colorado and California made friends with local youth, and in the evenings Mr. Salazar kept a watchful eye on his teenage granddaughters.

Early Sunday morning it was chilly, and ten-thirty found the session going in the open air, but only a few members occupied the folding chairs set in rows before the rough plank speakers' platform. They huddled in sheepskin coats and black wide-brimmed hats. A few hours later warm sunshine streamed down on cottonwood and piñon, and a crowd in shirtsleeves and cotton dresses filled the seats. Speakers warmed up also. "This is the land that will be ours. We will meet here a year from today." "The Lord willing," somebody prompts.

They were together in the sun, drawing strength from one another. A "human atmosphere" prevailed, remarked a young Chicano. They would build a city hall on this site, to impress all who passed with the visible existence of the community of San Joaquín. It would be used as a community center for the surrounding villages. Volunteers pledged lumber and "hours of work."

A guest from New Jersey, SNCC leader Phil Hutchings,

told the Alianzistas that to him, Tijerina was a symbol of "another alliance—the unity of the wretched of the earth, *los pobres de la tierra,* black, brown and bronze."

Later, the discussion centered around the possibility of regaining nearby land held by the Presbyterian Church, and this prospect was viewed with joy.

THE BURNING SIGNS

BILL HIGGS was accompanied by an heir to the Montgomery Ward millions from Chicago and by 19-year-old Mark Bralley, a photographer from Albuquerque, who later confessed to being an FBI agent. That morning Higgs drove this young man, together with a wire service reporter and the author, on a tour of Forest Service signs he said were targets for burning.

In the afternoon, Patsy Tijerina announced she wanted to burn a sign, and that she had the approval of Mayor Salazar.

The sign-burning came at the end of that weekend. Reies and Patsy went to the site in a clearing by the highway, accompanied by more than 150 people, including several press photographers. Patsy threw a bottle of gasoline at the 4 x 6 foot redwood sign that proclaimed "Santa Fe National Forest —US Department of Agriculture," and lit it. About 20 state policemen arrived on the scene and stood watching. Tijerina told them, "None of these people are violent, I am the only one who has a gun, and you know why I carry one. I was shot at the other night."

Suddenly, 15 Forest Rangers came swooping down a slope, brandishing automatic weapons, and surrounded Tijerina. Earlier, Patsy burned a sign at Gallinas, and the police had also been standing by. But Special Agent Evans was watching through binoculars and called the U.S. Attorney. Whatever decision was made, it was a political one.

Although Patsy was doing the burning, Evans, carrying a special carbine with a double cartridge clip, tried to grab Reies. A swarm of people got in between them, and Evans

Reies Tijerina at the Poor Peoples' March, Washington, D.C., 1968. *At the left:* Hank Adams and Al Bridges, Indian leaders; *at the right,* Rev. Ralph Abernathy.

backed off and then lunged forward, grabbing Reies by the belt. He held his carbine pointed straight at Tijerina, and little Isabel, standing on the seat of the car behind them, began to cry.

Reies, realizing that she would also be in danger should Evans fire, ran over and, picking up his rifle from the front seat, placed himself so that the child would not be in the line of fire. Evans ran and hid behind the car, and when he later accused Tijerina of pointing the rifle at him, he was forced to admit in court that Reies "would have had to shoot through the windshield and the rear window in order to shoot me."[1]

Eight people were arrested, including Patsy, Reies, his brother Ramón and son Reies, Jr. Again, strangely, none from the land-grant families was held.

Four leaders of SNCC spent the night in Santa Fe County jail, charged with being "parties to a crime." Overnight the charge was reduced to driving without a license, and when one was produced they were released, as were all others except Reies and Patsy Tijerina. The government had zeroed in on its target for the third time.

The day after they returned from Coyote, an Alianza delegation announced plans for a citizen's arrest of Special Agent Evans at his home near Albuquerque. Evans spent the night in a motel, and Tijerina did not go along with the plan. When the arrest was attempted, Bill Higgs declined to comment on Tijerina's whereabouts, or why he did not participate. But the Alianza action was sufficient for Evans to demand that Reies' bond be immediately revoked.

At the bond revocation hearing, Robert Gilliland, State Police criminal investigator who had been prominent in the events following the murder of Salazar, testified that he had aimed a shotgun at Tijerina's head and was thinking, "If Reies pulls that trigger, I'm going to shoot him." But Tijerina had put his gun down and surrendered.

"You really hate this man, don't you?" asked William Kunstler, Tijerina's lawyer.

"Yes, sir, I do," Gilliland replied. Gilliland said he had had Tijerina under surveillance for three years, and when Kunstler asked him if he had ever seen Tijerina strike anybody, or commit any act of violence during that period, Gilliland barked, "Every time he opens his mouth it's violence. He goes up north and spreads his crap around—I can't understand why he isn't in jail," said the man assigned to investigate the bombings at Alianza headquarters.[2]

Tijerina was sent to the penitentiary June 11, but Patsy was free on bond. At a preliminary hearing in July, Forest Ranger Evans was heard by reporters outside the courtroom to exclaim, "I would like to kill that bastard," with reference to Tijerina.

At the hearing, many Alianzistas who had been present at the sign burning took the stand, trying to explain that "all of our struggle is worth it for our land." "Don't get into any of this land stuff," admonished the judge.

"If the land doesn't belong to the Forest Service, the signs do," said the prosecutor. Tijerina was convicted of "assault on a Forest Ranger," and "aiding and abetting" the destruction of government property. The jury was all Anglo except for one postal employee, and testimony by expert witnesses on the background of the struggle for San Joaquín was not admitted.

Patsy was not tried until February, half a year later. The court-appointed lawyer appealed to a combination of racial and male superiority in seeking a defense. He pleaded that Patsy didn't have the mental capacity to know what she was doing when she burned the signs, but Patsy maintained that she had burned them because "the land belongs to the people. All the signs have to go down, and all the fences."

The same judge who convicted her husband for "aiding" Patsy in a crime that had not been proven when he was tried, placed her on five years' probation.

Reies' sentence was three years in the penitentiary. As he stood before the bench, Reies turned to see what the judge was staring at. The entire audience had risen to be sentenced with him.

SECOND TIERRA AMARILLA TRIAL

TIJERINA WAS tried twice on essentially the same charges derived from the events at Tierra Amarilla. He was acquitted the first time, convicted the second. What was the difference between the two trials?

The change from the evidence heard by the jury in the first trial to what the new jurors were allowed to hear in the second, ten months later, was craftily planned by Special Assistant Attorney General Jack Love. Love had wanted to become attorney general but lost the election, and now he had been appointed special assistant for the specific purpose of jailing Tijerina. He could not fail again. So prior to the second trial, Love wrote Judge Burks, urging him not to admit evidence that would give the jury the true picture of a man fighting for the rights and dignity of his people. The State would take the position, he said, that in connection with the forthcoming trial, "evidence as to the defendant's background, life history, and activities prior to the incident in question," were irrelevant, including "the purpose and history of the Alianza."

"The sociological and anthropological history of northern New Mexico; the law and history of land grants in northern New Mexico," would also be fought as inadmissable, as well as "the conduct and activities of former District Attorney Alfonso Sanchez, and other law enforcement officers, prior to the incident in question.

"Second, we urge that the defendant himself be prohibited from conducting *voir dire* (questioning) of prospective jurors."

Although the motives of the State in trying to imprison him were purely political, Tijerina's motives would be presented as those of a common criminal.

And, in asking the judge to bar essential evidence, Love was admitting that if given all the facts, the new jury would again find Tijerina's actions justifiable. When denied the right to question the jury, as he had done with considerable insight in the first trial, Tijerina was being deprived of an opportunity to uncover—and in some cases mitigate—their racist attitudes.

The land-grant leader had been in jail since June 11, his bond revoked on petition from "Jungle Jim" Evans. During that time he had conducted his own defense on the charge of burning Forest Service signs at Coyote.

In October he faced more charges stemming from the Tierra Amarilla incident, and before the trial began, state and federal officials worked together to subject him to a cruel ordeal. Reies had at first been placed in solitary confinement in La Tuna Federal Prison near El Paso, Texas, but after a week was shifted to the Albuquerque City jail, then after another week transferred to Santa Fe, then back to Albuquerque, then again transferred to Santa Fe, again to La Tuna, again to Albuquerque City jail, then to Santa Fe and back to La Tuna, then back to Santa Fe. "It was clear that they did all this to torment my mind and to keep me from adequately preparing my defense," he wrote. "I had told the court that I intended to act as my own attorney (again) and they were raging mad."[3]

He was able to interview prospective witnesses only through a small opening in a steel door and to see only those whose names appeared on a list provided by U.S. Marshal Naranjo, father of Río Arriba County Sheriff Benny Naranjo, and leader of the Democratic machine that so strongly opposed him.

He was not only denied the facilities needed to prepare for a trial, but the pressure of whirlwind shifting, always in solitary confinement, told on Reies' health. He was suffering from severe headaches, and appeared for this trial looking ill, his customary muscle tone and quick, energetic responses dulled. And this time Attorney Axelrod was not there to point up flaws in the State's evidence, and help sharpen the arguments for defense.

The weekend before the trial, the Alianza held its annual convention, and since he was in Albuquerque City Jail, Reies was able to discuss the proceedings with visitors. But without consulting him, the convention made a far-reaching departure from Alianza policy. It passed a resolution that asked President Nixon to permit the establishment of an independent nation in the Southwest, in the territory seized from Mexico. "The population and area estimates came from Bill Higgs," said the *Journal* (October 23, 1969).

The plan was an extreme version of the *Plan Espiritual de Aztlán*—Spiritual Plan of Aztlán—a declaration of support for cultural autonomy put forth by the Denver Crusade for Justice and adopted by a conference of 1,500 youth: "With our heart in our hands and our hands in the soil, we declare the independence of the Mestizo Nation. . . . We are a nation, we are a union of free Pueblos, we are Aztlán."[4]

Harassed and tense from the strain of preparing his defense in a jail cell, Tijerina exploded. He refused to endorse the Alianza resolution, which went far beyond that adopted in Denver, and announced he was resigning as president. He was not in favor of "separatism from the United States," he said, but was instead fighting for equal status within the nation. "My motto is justice, but not independence from the government of the United States." Ramón Tijerina, elected to serve in his brother's stead, said the plan was "all new to him when presented at the convention," but that he would support it.

For Reies, it had been frustrating to sit in jail while the Alianza met in convention. Now he was further disturbed, because the resolution calling for a separate nation would certainly create divisions where he now most needed support, in the Indo-Hispano population that makes up one-third of the State's people.

His resignation came on the same day the second Tierra Amarilla trial began. The State had declared they would prosecute Tijerina, three charges at a time, until they got a jury that would convict him. As the trial opened, Attorney Mort Stavis accused the prosecution of "a barbarous attempt to try the defendant piecemeal, wear down his resistance, and build up a greater case against him by the use of public opinion." Tijerina asked to be tried on all 20 charges at once, and with his nine co-defendants. By trying them separately the State was obtaining convictions by clear and blatant conflicts in their evidence in each successive proceeding.

These motions were denied, but the trial got off to a false start when, on the second day, a woman juror and bailiff Ida Maynard were seen drinking in the bar of the Hilton Hotel with sports promoter Mike London. Oddly enough, Mrs. Maynard had been bailiff for the jury in Tijerina's previous trials, both State and Federal. There was a strong suggestion of an attempted payoff, but the details were hushed up and a mistrial declared.

The trial began again. The most serious charge against Tijerina was that of assaulting the jailer, Salazar, with intent to kill him. There were no witnesses to the shooting of Salazar, and Sheriff Naranjo had told Station KOB's Bill Leverton immediately after the event, "I heard a shot in the hallway, and my jailer (Salazar) says 'get the hell out of here,' and he jumped out of the window and they shot him outside the window." At the time, the *New Mexican* (June 11, 1967) also had reported that the jailer "was struck twice by bullets as he landed on the sidewalk in front of the courthouse." No written statement was made by Salazar.

In this trial Naranjo declared that Tijerina had gone into the sheriff's office and "shot Salazar in the face as the jailer leaped out of the window." This acrobatic feat was never explained. Saíz, who was flat on his back in the courthouse lobby when the jailer was shot, also now changed his story and said he had seen Tijerina going into the sheriff's office. He didn't know why he had not mentioned it before. Tijerina denied that he entered the sheriff's office the day of the raid.

The first person to talk to Salazar after he was shot was Mrs. Rosemary Mercure of Tierra Amarilla, who said that she spoke to Salazar outside the courthouse and that he was bleeding. "I said, 'Godfather, what happened?' and he said, '*Los Ti-jerinas,** they shot me.' "

Cross-examined, Mrs. Mercure said Salazar did not identify Tijerina himself, but that *Los Tijerinas* could refer to anybody.

Placido Mercure, the husband of Rosemary, also heard Eulogio say *Los Tijerinas,* he testified. "When you heard *Los Tijerinas,* who did you think they were referring to?" "The whole bunch—the people."

In desperation, Love brought in 11 of Salazar's relatives, who told of visiting the jailer one at a time in the hospital. Each claimed to have asked him the same question: "Who did it?" According to all eleven, Salazar, whose jaw was bandaged, took a slip of paper 11 different times and wrote on it the word "Tijerina." Not one of them, not even his widow or three daughters, showed the note to the others, and not one saved the note. Spectators felt they were watching an old-fashioned drive for blood revenge. Several of the young girls were so nervous that Tijerina did not cross-examine them, nor did he question Mrs. Salazar.

But Love cashed in on the atmosphere of superstitious fear he had created, befuddling the jury into thinking that the wounding of Salazar at Tierra Amarilla and his murder six months later were somehow the same event. He closed his speech to the jury with, "We ask you not to come in here and say Eulogio Salazar died a liar."

Although the jury found Tijerina guilty of assaulting Salazar, they did not accept the second charge, that he had "falsely imprisoned" Jaramillo, who by then had succeeded Naranjo as sheriff of Río Arriba County.

Attached to the verdict was a note: "We feel that although he did commit the acts, his motives were different than what was implied by the State."

A juror later explained, "It was like a man who breaks the

* Popular form of reference to the Alianza or to any supporter of Tijerina.

speed laws taking his wife to the hospital to have a baby. We feel Tijerina may have told them to go into the commissioner's room, but it was for their own safety."

15. The End Hasn't Been Written Yet*

THE NEAREST the Alianza has yet come to recovering their grant lands was from the Presbyterian Church in May and June 1969. The grant involved was the Piedra Lumbre (Flint) Grant in Río Arriba county, and the land was the area known as Ghost Ranch, owned by the church, and adjacent to the San Joaquín grant.

Religious bodies had had their consciences jolted that Spring by the Black Manifesto of James Foreman, accusing the Christian sects of ignoring the needy and demanding "reparations" for the victims of their neglect.

The Presbyterians are the owners of several tracts in northern New Mexico, and in May the general assembly of the United Presbyterian Church, meeting in San Antonio, Texas, voted to return to the people of the area 20,000 acres of the Piedra Lumbre grant, which the church held by gift from a former possessor.

Tijerina addressed the assembly and traced the unconscionable means by which the grant had fallen into the hands of the church, and delegates were shocked to hear that the name "Ghost Ranch" came from the fact that the land had no title. It was assumed that the Alianza, as the organization represent-

* Closing line of Juan Roybal's *Corrida de Río Arriba*.

ing the land-grant heirs, would be the receiver of the property the church meant to release. To prevent any such thing from happening, Bob Brown, editor of the Albuquerque *Journal* and a prominent Presbyterian, excoriated Tijerina and submitted an amendment, which was passed, to provide that negotiations on the land would be with "local Spanish-American leaders" rather than with "a recognized Spanish-American organization."

In essence, Brown's private appeal to the Presbyterians was along the following lines:

"Do not get carried away by sentiment and make a concession to the Alianza. If these people succeed in anything, they will overturn New Mexico, and everything that we hold dear will be lost. Their movement threatens the existing base of power, and this we must preserve. Justice regarding the Piedra Lumbre grant has nothing to do with the case. The Alianza must be defeated."

On June 1, more than 300 members of the Alianza, led by Tijerina, confronted about 100 delegates to the Synod of the United Presbyterian Church being held at the Ghost Ranch. They were expected, and met with tea, cookies, and a three-page, single-spaced position paper. "The Church will move to exercise its deep concern for the progress of the Spanish-speaking people, but it will do so on its own terms. . . ." Tijerina and five other speakers called for the Presbyterians to recognize the Alianza as representatives of the legitimate heirs. Tijerina accused Brown of carrying out a personal feud with him at the Church convention. "More than 300 families are expected to be affected by your decision," he said. "These people want to own the land in common."

Celestino Velasquez, chairman of the Piedra Lumbre grant, told the Synod that "The people will accept the Alianza, because the Alianza is made up of the heirs, and is the only organization fighting for their land."

All the land-grant speakers said they would never accept appointed administrators of the released land.

A cash grant of $50,000 for the development of the land was voted at San Antonio to accompany the land transfer. Neither land nor money was conveyed, however, as the church spokesmen refused to recognize the Alianza as the representative of the heirs, and the "group of Spanish-American leaders" which they said they would find to receive the gifts was never assembled. The church must have discovered very soon that any such group in the area could only consist of Alianza members.

The mouse which finally was born from the mountain was an offer to let the Alianza use the extensive Ghost Ranch buildings, owned by the church, for a seminar on community leadership. That never took place either.

The Episcopal Church had also received the message. The church's executive council, meeting in December in Greenwich, Connecticut and over the strenuous protest of the Rt. Rev. Charles J. Kinsolving III, bishop of New Mexico and West Texas, voted the Alianza a $40,000 grant for community development.

Bishop Kinsolving condemned the action as aiding an organization dedicated to "violence". He announced that his diocese would withhold its payments to the "missionary quota" of the national church, amounting to over $80,000 for the following year. New Mexico sent its official State archivist and historian, Myra Ellen Jenkins, to try to get the ear of powerful churchmen and head off the Alianza grant.

But a staff report to the Episcopal council on the Alianza's request for funds, after noting the opposition of Bishop Kinsolving and the grounds for it, continued, "not one church in New Mexico has ever acted in a manner which would force serious consideration of the Alianza position. It is therefore sheer hypocrisy to speak of 'law and order' and 'violence.' The indifference of responsible whites in New Mexico compelled the leadership of the Alianza to employ confrontation tactics."

Some Episcopalian cash actually was received by the Alianza after Tijerina's imprisonment, and spent to buy a printing press and to keep the Alianza going in his absence.

On the same day that Tijerina's bond was revoked, the Ford Foundation announced a $1.5 million feedlot loan to benefit the poor of northern New Mexico. This was not the Foundation's first initiative in New Mexico. Its first direct contact was in the Spring of 1967, when former Governor Campbell encouraged Ford to come into New Mexico to put down Tijerina. Within a month after Tierra Amarilla, a team was dispatched to New Mexico to divert attention from Tijerina and the land question by creating an alternative leader as quickly as possible.

Ford granted half a million dollars to start the program to knock out Tijerina. The man groomed for "alternative leadership" was Alex Mercure of the Home Education Livelihood Program, and when Congress called hearings after the Tierra Amarilla incident it called Mercure to testify, not Tijerina or the Alianzistas.[1]

Money poured into the North. But Gilberto Ballejos, editor of *El Papel* in Albuquerque, exposed Ford's move; "They're trying to create *Vendido* Power (sellout power) . . . trying to bring Vietnam to New Mexico and trying to create 'leaders' the system can use as tools. But it hasn't worked with the Vietnamese and it's not going to work with Raza here in the United States."[2]

In August 1970, Mercure charged that the HELP program had been "frozen out" of running the Ford feedlot, and that the feedlot was being operated in Colorado for the benefit of big cattlemen, with no Mexicans in decision-making positions.[3]

But a cooperative was organized in Tierra Amarilla, without Ford or Federal money. Tijerina's years of patient effort in the Tierra Amarilla area have not yet won back the land, but they have produced a valuable by-product: the people's increased confidence that they can help themselves. Twenty families who joined their land together and built the agricultural cooperative have survived their second year. With the help of volunteer youth from Colorado and as far away as France, and with tractors bought with funds contributed from Albuquerque to Connecticut, they have worked together to grow food that nourishes their large families through the winter.

Tierra Amarilla children are now receiving free dental care from a cooperative clinic run by land-grant heirs, who are also providing medical attention in this country where there was no doctor for 50 miles, where 16 out of every 100 babies died in their first year.

Their efforts have been made more difficult by the hostility of big ranchers—arsonists burned the clinic in September 1969 when it was about to open, but the villagers pitched in to rebuild, and funds were raised to replace thousands of dollars worth of medicines and equipment destroyed in the fire.

Another reason New Mexico's big ranchers wish Tijerina behind bars is that he has given small farmers the courage to seek out documents proving their ownership to the land. Such a case involves the claimants to 4,000 acres now occupied by E. E. Fogelson, husband of Greer Garson, where the film star queens it over an extensive spread behind fences painted a bright pink. Fogelson, who controls the ranch from Texas, won a temporary injunction in June 1969 against Esquipula Padilla, enjoining him against "trespassing" on the pastures of the Forked Lightning Ranch near Las Vegas, N. M. Fogelson's men have attacked local families more than once, when the latter tried to take their children to a school located on land the rancher claimed.

The wealthy Fogelson's attorney, John S. Catron, said his client's ownership would be proven, not by title but by "adverse possession" for a decade.

The Padilla family has run livestock on those pastures for four generations that they know of, and Mr. Padilla explained the copy of an 1887 quit-claim he had just got from the County files with the assistance of the District Attorney. Sitting in the small, neat kitchen of his farm, Mr. Padilla said that they had protested Fogelson's use of their land for years, but not since the Alianza had begun to develop political power had they been able to get hold of documents necessary to prove ownership. The case is pending in the courts.

A few of the militants who came to the northern counties attracted by Tijerina's fight, have stayed to establish a paper, *El Grito del Norte* (Cry of the North). It has not yet been taken over by the people of the villages, as its founders planned, but it is giving some of them valuable experience and a vehicle for expressing their grievances. It also brings news to the North of the Chicano movement burgeoning in the rest of the Southwest, and contributes to a sense of unity with their struggling brothers.

The shots fired in the courthouse raid are still echoing. Tobias Leyba, Moises Morales, José Madríl and Salomon Velasquez still face trials, and the convictions of Juan Valdez and Geronimo Borunda are pending appeal as this is written, as is that of Tijerina.

The climate in which they are tried may be helped by a plan of the Alianza to submit the legality of the land grants to a public tribunal, patterned after Bertrand Russell's War Crimes Trial. Prominent judges, including lawyers and historians, from Europe and Latin America are being asked to hear testimony in New Mexico in order to determine whether the claims of Indo-Hispanos are valid. If successful, the tribunal will have a powerful moral impact, that could reverberate throughout the Southwest as did the alarm sounded at Tierra Amarilla.

As this is written, friends and relatives of Tijerina are preparing to meet him at the prison gates in Springfield, Mo. where he is being released on parole, his health damaged after more than two years in the penitentiary.

Another sentence still hangs over him. It stems from the

second Tierra Amarilla trial and is on appeal in the State courts. As part of a move to ask the Governor to commute this sentence, petitions are being circulated that read:

"Some people argue that salting Mr. Tijerina away in jail is the best way of keeping things quiet in New Mexico, but we say that this is not true. Putting a cork on real grievances only makes the grievances grow. We feel that *freedom now* for Mr. Tijerina is in the best interests of our State."

Legislation requested by the Alianza has been introduced in the U.S. House by Representative Augustus Hawkins of California. It calls for a probe of the Treaty of Guadalupe Hidalgo by a Federal commission set up to determine the validity of land claims based on the Treaty's guarantees. Senator Fred Harris of Oklahoma has agreed to support this bill.

If a genuine study of land tenure in New Mexico as provided by the Treaty is actually made, it can help bring about a new era in the Southwest in which deeply rooted injustices are at last brought to an end.

FROM LETTERS WRITTEN IN PRISON BY
REIES LOPEZ TIJERINA*

(no date)
What has inspired me against racism: the disastrous danger represented by racism; its anti-human effect that lessens all of humanity, is what has moved me. The bloody dimensions that race hatred reveals, is awakening all truly wise men.

April 2, 1970
My son, never for any reason allow hatred to dominate your life.

April 10, 1970
Your heart begins to feel that the suffering of the other prisoners is more tormenting to your soul than the bars to

* By permission of Reies Hugh "David" Tijerina. Translation by the author.

your body. Some prisoners are very strong by nature, and able to hide the pain in their hearts. But for how long? Others are not so strong, they water the prison with their tears, and from their hearts escape such cries that even the brave tremble.

This is my prison, son, this is the world in which I am now living. I want to do more to help those who need it, and in a word contribute to peace and understanding among the peoples.

APPENDIX

INSTRUCTIONS ON THE RIGHT OF CITIZENS' ARREST GIVEN BY THE COURT IN THE CASE OF THE STATE OF NEW MEXICO V. REIES TIJERINA *(abbreviated)*

The Court instructs the Jury that citizens of New Mexico have the right to make a citizens' arrest under the following circumstances:

If the arresting person reasonably believes that the person arrested, or attempted to be arrested, was the person who committed, either as a principal, or as an aider and abettor, a felony; . . .

The Court instructs the Jury that a citizens' arrest can be made even though distant in time and place from the acts constituting or reasonably appearing to constitute the commission of the felony. The Court further instructs the Jury that a citizens' arrest may be made whether or not law enforcement officers are present. . . .

The Court instructs the Jury that any one, including a State Police Officer, who intentionally interferes with a lawful attempt to make a citizens' arrest does so at his peril, since the arresting citizens are entitled under the law to use whatever force is reasonably necessary. . . .

Authorities:

Holdsworth's *History of the Law of England,* Arrest; Territory v. McGinnis, 10 New Mexico Reports 26, (1900); 6 Corpus Juris Secundum, Arrest, Sections 8 *et seq.;* Alexander, *The Law of Arrest,* Section 50.

(Comment: A conspiracy or concerted action to deny citizens of the United States their Constitutional rights is a federal felony carrying a punishment upon conviction of a maximum of 10 years in prison and/or $5,000 fine. Title 18, *United States Code,* Section 241.)

Reference Notes

CHAPTER 1

1. Mario Gill, *Nuestros Buenos Vecinos,* Editorial Azteca, Mexico, 1964, p. 19.
2. Glenn W. Price, *Origins of the War with Mexico,* Univ. of Texas Press, Austin, 1967, p. 17.
3. Gill, *op. cit.,* p. 18.
4. Carey McWilliams, *North from Mexico,* Greenwood Press, New York, 1968, p. 20.
5. Gill, *op. cit.,* p. 46.
6. *Personal Memoirs of Gen. U.S. Grant,* C. L. Webster, New York, 1894, pp. 54–55, 68.
7. Price, *op. cit.,* p. 89.
8. *Survey of the Modern and Contemporary History of Mexico,* Alperovich and Iavrov, eds., Moscow, 1960.
9. José Fernando Ramirez, *Mexico Durante Su Guerra,* documentos inéditos, Mexico City, 1847.
10. William A. Keleher, *Turmoil in New Mexico 1846–1868,* Rydal Press, Santa Fe, 1952, p. 17.
11. *Occupation of New Mexico,* Beier, ed., Southwest Historical Series III, Glendale, Calif., 1935, p. 205.
12. *Ibid.*
13. George Sanchez, *Forgotten People,* Calvin Horn, Albuquerque, 1969, p. 16.
14. Price, *op. cit.* p. 165.
15. Gill, *op. cit.,* p. 62.
16. *U.S. State Department Document 129,* Washington D.C., 1848, p. 375–76.
17. Mariano Otero, *Exposición Sobre la Guerra 1847,* Matiano, Mexico City, 1947, pp. 48–61.
18. Ralph E. Twitchell, *The Leading Facts of New Mexico History,* The Torch Press, Cedar Rapids, 1912, Vol. II, p. 311.
19. Karl Marx and Frederick Engels, *The Civil War in the United States,* International Publishers, New York, 1969, pp. 64, 297.
20. Albuquerque *Journal,* October 29, 1967.

Chapter 2

1. Gill, *op. cit.*, p. 71.
2. Anne M. Smith, *New Mexico Indians*, New Mexico Research Record No. 1–1966, Santa Fe, 1966.
3. Jack Holmes, *Politics in New Mexico*, Univ. of New Mexico Press, Albuquerque, 1967, p. 33.
4. Matthew Edel, *The Mexican Ejido: Revolution and Land Reform*, Cambridge Institute Occasional Bulletin, October 1969. Reprinted in *New Mexico Review*, March 1970, p. 5.
5. Horacio Ulibarrí, *The Effect of Cultural Difference in the Education of Spanish Americans*, Univ. of New Mexico Research Study *(mimeographed)*, 1958, p. 56.
6. Margaret Mead, *Cultural Patterns and Technical Change*, World Federation of Mental Health, New York, 1955, p. 153.
7. New York *Herald*, January 30, 1848, in Albert K. Weinburg, *Manifest Destiny*, John Hopkins, Baltimore, 1935, p. 90.
8. Ulibarrí, *op. cit.*, p. 57.
9. Victor Westphall, *The Public Domain in New Mexico 1854–1891*, Univ. of New Mexico Press, Albuquerque, 1966, p. 54.
10. George Bancroft, *History of Arizona and New Mexico*, 1885, p. 717.
11. Frances Swadesh, "Review of *Land Grant Problems in New Mexico*," *New Mexico Review*, January 1970, p. 3.
12. Twitchell, *op. cit.*, p. 467.
13. *Congressional Record*, 78th Congress, Second Session, Washington D.C., May 12, 1946.
14. Howard Roberts Lamar, *The Far Southwest 1846–1912*, Yale Univ. Press, New Haven, 1966, p. 17, 487.
15. Frances Swadesh, *Hispanic Americans of the Ute Frontier*, Research Report No. 50, Tri-Ethnic Cultural Project, Univ. of Colorado, *unpublished doctoral dissertation*.
16. Albuquerque *Tribune*, February 20, 1968.

Chapter 3

1. President's Committee on Civil Rights, Washington D.C., May 14, 1947.
2. *Mañana*, Mexico City, October 23, 1944.

3. Tony Hillerman, "The U.S. Stole Our Land," *True Magazine,* January 1968.

4. Clark S. Knowlton, Texas *Observer,* March 28, 1969.

5. Gill, *op. cit.,* p. 87.

6. Frances Swadesh, "The Alianza Movement," *Minorities and Politics,* Tobias and Woodhouse, eds., Univ. of New Mexico Press, Albuquerque, 1969, p. 69.

7. Reies Tijerina, *The Spanish Land Grant Question Examined,* Alianza Federal, Albuquerque, 1966.

Chapter 4

1. Albuquerque *News-Chieftain,* September 7, 1963.

2. Knowlton, *Land Grant Problems Among the State's Spanish-Americans,* Univ. of New Mexico Bureau of Business Research *(Mimeographed),* 1967.

3. Peter Nabokov, Santa Fe *New Mexican,* February 4, 1968.

4. Knowlton, *op. cit.*

5. Hubert Kaufman, *The Forest Ranger,* John Hopkins Press, Baltimore, 1960, p. 57.

6. Albuquerque *Journal,* January 23, 1969.

7. *Mineral Industry Surveys,* U.S. Bureau of Mines, Washington D.C., 1968.

8. Albuquerque *Journal,* November 5, 1969.

9. Morris Garnsey, "The Future of the Mountain States," *Harper's Magazine,* October 1945.

10. Cecil V. Romero, "The Riddle of the Adobe," *New Mexico Historical Review,* October 1929.

11. Kaufman, *op. cit.,* p. 197, 205.

12. Swadesh, *Hispanic Americans of the Ute Frontier,* Tri-Ethnic Research Project, Univ. of Colorado, *(unpublished)* Research Report No. 50, p. 309.

13. William O. Douglas, *Points of Rebellion,* Vintage Books, New York, 1970, p. 78.

14. Albuquerque *Journal,* December 15, 1967.

15. Las Cruces *Sun-News,* April 12, 1971.

16. John Ise, *The U.S. Forest Policy,* Yale Univ. Press, New Haven, 1926, p. 167

17. House Agricultural Subcommittee Hearings, Denver *Post,* June 14, 1967.

18. Santa Fe *New Mexican,* August 25, 1967.

CHAPTER 5

    1. Holmes, *op. cit.,* p. 52.
    2. Albuquerque *Journal,* July 4, 1966.
    3. Mark Acuff, Santa Fe *New Mexican,* July 6, 1966.

CHAPTER 6

    1. El Paso *Times,* November 6, 1967.
    2. Albuquerque *Journal,* February 20, 1967.
    3. Albuquerque *Journal,* June 2, 1969.

CHAPTER 7

    1. Albuquerque *Herald Tribune,* March 15, 1968.

CHAPTER 8

    1. Santa Fe *New Mexican,* June 6, 1967.
    2. William Olson, "Fun and Games at Tierra Amarilla," *Irregular Review,* August 1967.
    3. Santa Fe *New Mexican,* June 8, 1967.
    4. Santa Fe *New Mexican,* June 12, 1967.
    5. Santa Fe *New Mexican,* June 15, 1967.
    6. Albuquerque *Journal,* June 15, 1967.
    7. Albuquerque *Journal,* June 14, 1967.
    8. Albuquerque *Journal,* June 15, 1967.
    9. *Ibid.*
    10. Albuquerque *Journal,* August 8, 1967.
    11. *The New York Times,* June 22, 1967.
    12. Swadesh, "The Alianza Movement: Catalyst for Social Change in New Mexico," Proceedings of Meeting of the American Ethnological Society, Univ. of Washington Press, 1968, p. 172.
    13. Ed Meagher, Los Angeles *Times,* February 4, 1968.

CHAPTER 9

    1. Albuquerque *Journal,* June 18, 1967.
    2. Santa Fe *New Mexican,* July 6, 1967.
    3. Albuquerque *Journal,* December 6, 1967.

4. Santa Fe *New Mexican,* July 6, 1967.
5. *People's World,* January 20, 1968.
6. Albuquerque *Journal,* December 29, 1967.
7. *El Gallo,* January 1968.
8. Albuquerque *Journal,* January 9, 1968.

CHAPTER 10

1. Albuquerque *Journal,* May 21, 1969.
2. Albuquerque *Journal,* July 13, 1968.
3. *U.S. Census, 1960,* for percentage Spanish surnames.
4. *Low Income Families in the Spanish Surnamed Population of the Southwest.* USDA Economic Research Series No. 112, 1967, p. 14.
5. *The Hired Farm Working Force,* USDA Economic Report No. 98, 1966, p. 6.
6. *US Government Organization Manual,* Washington D.C., July 1, 1970, p. 252.
7. Santa Fe *New Mexican,* April 1, 1968.
8. John H. Burma and David E. Williams, *An Economic, Social and Educational Survey of Rio Arriba and Táos Counties, unpublished report* in State Archives, 1960.
9. Washington *Post,* June 5, 1968.
10. *US News and World Report,* May 27, 1968.
11. "Summary Report of National Conference on Poverty in the Southwest," Phoenix, January 25–26, 1965, *(mimeographed)*.
12. *El Papel,* Albuquerque, May 1968.
13. *Southern Patriot,* May 1968.

CHAPTER 11

1. Santa Fe *New Mexican,* June 5, 1968.

CHAPTER 12

1. Washington *Sunday Star,* June 16, 1968.
2. *Statistical Yearbook,* UNESCO, New York, 1969, p. 23.

CHAPTER 13

1. *Lobo,* University of New Mexico, September 25, 1968.
2. Wayne S. Scott, *Albuquerque Journal,* October 26, 1968.

3. Albuquerque *Journal,* May 29, 1970.
4. Albuquerque *Journal,* December 24, 1968.
5. Albuquerque *Journal,* December 11, 1968.
6. *La Voz Norteña,* June 1967.
7. Albuquerque *Journal,* January 1969.

Chapter 14

1. *El Papel,* September 1969.
2. Albuquerque *Tribune,* June 17, 1969.
3. Tijerina, "A Letter From Jail, Santa Fe, August 15–17," *El Grito del Norte,* September 26, 1969.
4. Albuquerque *Tribune,* March 27, 1969.

Chapter 15

1. Rees Lloyd and Peter Montague, "Ford and La Raza," *Ramparts,* September 1970.
2. *El Papel,* April 1970.
3. Albuquerque Journal, August 25, 1970.

Index